Portuguese
Phrases
FOR
DUMMIES

by Karen Keller

Wiley Publishing, Inc.

Portuguese Phrases For Dummies®

Published by
Wiley Publishing, Inc.
111 River St.
Hoboken, NJ 07030-5774
www.wiley.com

For general information on our other products and services, please contact our Customer Care Department within the U.S. at 800-762-2974, outside the U.S. at 317-572-3993, or fax 317-572-4002.

For technical support, please visit www.wiley.com/techsupport.

Wiley also publishes its books in a variety of electronic formats. Some content that appears in print may not be available in electronic books.

Library of Congress Control Number: 2006936747

ISBN: 978-0-470-03750-8

Manufactured in the United States of America

10 9 8 7 6 5 4 3 2 1

1O/QY/RS/QW/IN

About the Author

Karen Keller is a journalist who lived and worked in
São Paulo, Brazil, for three years. Before moving to
Brazil, the California native taught Spanish at a New
York City–based foreign-language-education Web site.
Keller is also a published travel-guide writer. She cur-
rently lives in New Jersey, where she is a local news-
paper reporter.

Publisher's Acknowledgments

We're proud of this book; please send us your comments through our Dummies online registration form located at www.dummies.com/register/.

Some of the people who helped bring this book to market include the following:

Acquisitions, Editorial, and Media Development

Compiler:
Laura Peterson-Nussbaum

Project Editor:
Elizabeth Kuball

Acquisitions Editor:
Stacy Kennedy

Technical Editor:
Fernanda Habermann

Editorial Manager:
Michelle Hacker

Consumer Editorial Supervisor and Reprint Editor:
Carmen Krikorian

Editorial Assistants:
Erin Calligan,
David Lutton

Cartoons: Rich Tennant,
www.the5thwave.com

Composition

Project Coordinator:
Patrick Redmond

Layout and Graphics:
Stephanie D. Jumper,
Erin Zeltner

Proofreaders:
Mildred Rosenzweig

Indexer: Stephen Ingle

Publishing and Editorial for Consumer Dummies

Diane Graves Steele, Vice President and Publisher, Consumer Dummies

Joyce Pepple, Acquisitions Director, Consumer Dummies

Kristin A. Cocks, Product Development Director, Consumer Dummies

Michael Spring, Vice President and Publisher, Travel

Kelly Regan, Editorial Director, Travel

Publishing for Technology Dummies

Andy Cummings, Vice President and Publisher, Dummies Technology/General User

Composition Services

Gerry Fahey, Vice President of Production Services

Debbie Stailey, Director of Composition Services

Table of Contents

The 5th Wave

By Rich Tennant

"Is there an easy phrase in Portuguese for removing a squid from a cowboy hat that won't make me look like a tourist?"

Introduction

The world is shrinking. Communication technology is getting faster and faster, making it easier to contact people in what used to be exotic, faraway lands. Air travel has gotten a lot cheaper, too, so visiting these places has never been simpler. Experiencing **um pouco** (oong *poh*-koo; a little) of a new language is a great way to familiarize yourself with a region of the world or specific country. Not only does it allow you to communicate verbally, but knowing new words opens the door to understanding the specific culture itself.

If you're curious about language and want to know how to ask someone's name, ask for directions in a city, or talk about what your interests are, you've come to the right place. I'm not promising fluency here, but this book provides a great start.

This book tells you about the language spoken in Brazil. Thanks to Brazil's huge population — around 170 million or so — Portuguese is the fifth-most-spoken language in the world. (Flip ahead to Chapter 1 to read about which other countries in the world speak Portuguese.)

Brazilian Portuguese is specific because the accent and some basic words are unique to Brazil. And the country itself is a pretty popular destination these days, with its earned reputation as a land of fun-loving, generous people.

A bonus to knowing Brazilian Portuguese is that it can help you to understand a little French, Spanish, and Italian, too. They're all Romance languages, which means many words among these languages sound similar.

Brazilian Portuguese is very lyrical. The sounds can be difficult to make for nonnative speakers, but speaking Portuguese is fun after you get into it. I advise you to treat yourself while you're reading the book: Buy some Brazilian music. You'll fall in love with the sounds, and the background music adds great ambience.

About This Book

Here's the good news: This book isn't a class you have to drag yourself to. It's a reference book, so use it at your leisure. You're the boss. You may choose to just leaf through, glancing only at chapters and pages that grab your attention. Or you can read the whole thing from start to finish. (From finish to start is okay, too — no one's looking.)

The first few chapters may be helpful to read first, though, because they explain some basic information about pronunciation and explain words that appear throughout the book.

Conventions Used in This Book

To make the book easy to read and understand, I've set up a few stylistic rules:

- ✔ Web addresses appear in monofont.

- ✔ Portuguese terms are set in **boldface** to make them stand out.

- ✔ Pronunciations and definitions, which are shown in parentheses, follow the terms the first time they appear in a section.

- ✔ Within the pronunciation, the part of the word that's stressed is shown in *italics*.

- ✔ Knowing key words and phrases is important in the quest to speak a new language. I collect important words and put them in a special blackboard-shaped "Words to Know" box.

> ✔ Verb conjugations (lists that show you the forms of a verb) are given in tables in this order: the *I* form, the *you* form, the *he/she* form, the *we* form, and the *they* form. Pronunciations follow in a second column.

Here's an example of a conjugation chart for the word **ser** (seh; to be). Because the subjects always come in the same order, you can see that words in this chart mean *I am, you are, he/she is, we are,* and *they are.*

Conjugation	Pronunciation
eu sou	*eh*-ooh *soh*
você é	voh-*seh eh*
ele/ela	*eh*-lee/*eh*-la *eh*
nós somos	*nohz soh*-mooz
eles/elas são	*eh*-leez/*eh*-lahz *sah*-ooh

Foolish Assumptions

To write this book, I had to imagine who my readers would be. Yes, you! I think if you've picked up this book, you're probably a pretty open-minded person who enjoys learning. That's excellent. Because the first step to absorbing new information is wanting to absorb it.

Here are some other things I'm imagining about you:

> ✔ You don't want to memorize long lists of vocabulary to know Portuguese.

> ✔ You want to get your feet wet in Portuguese while having fun at the same time.

> ✔ You're interested in learning about Brazilian culture as well as its language.

> ✔ You're not looking for a book to make you fluent in Portuguese but one that instead gives you bite-size information that provides a solid base to understanding the language.

Icons Used in This Book

Drawings and symbols always liven things up a bit, don't they? Here are some icons that point you to important information:

This icon shows you where you can find some fascinating tidbits that highlight either a linguistic aspect or give travel tips. Tips can save you time and frustration.

This handy icon pops up whenever you run across a bit of information that you really should remember after you close the book, whether it's about the Portuguese language or Brazil in general.

Languages are full of quirks that may trip you up if you're not prepared for them. This icon points to discussions of these weird grammar rules.

The "Cultural Wisdom" snippets help give insight into Brazilian culture.

Where to Go from Here

When you have a spare moment, pop open the book. All you need is a curious mind and the openness to learn about Brazil. Above all, don't think of reading the book as a chore. It's meant to be relaxing and enjoyable.

Feel free to complement this book with other activities that enhance your knowledge of Portuguese, like entering a Portuguese-language chat room on the Internet or having Brazilian music on in the background so you can hear the sounds of the language.

Oh, and **boa sorte** (*boh*-ah *soh*-chee; good luck)!

Chapter 1

Say It How? Speaking Portuguese

*B*elieve it or not, the Portuguese language comes in different versions. Pronunciation of Brazilian Portuguese and Portuguese from Portugal, say, is totally different. Some Brazilian tourists in Portugal report that they don't understand a word! I think it's a little more of a stretch than the differences between American and British English, just to give you an idea. But if a group of people from Texas, South Africa, and Scotland got together, they'd probably scratch their heads when trying to understand each other, too!

Written Portuguese, on the other hand, is very standard, especially when it's in a newspaper or some formal publication that doesn't use slang. A Brazilian can understand a Portuguese newspaper or read the works of Portugal's Nobel Prize–winning author José Saramago, no problem.

In this book, I focus on Brazilian Portuguese, as opposed to the Portuguese spoken in Portugal and countries in Africa — Cape Verde (islands off northwestern Africa), Mozambique (on the coast of southeast Africa), Guinea-Bissau (in western Africa), Angola (in southwestern Africa), and São Tomé and Príncipe (islands off western Africa).

Exploring the Roots of Portuguese

The beautiful Portuguese language belongs to a linguistic family known as the Romance languages. Back when the Roman Empire was around, Rome was in the center of a wide swath of Europe, northern Africa, and parts of Asia. With Rome's influence came its language — Latin.

And the closer a place was to Rome, the more likely it was to absorb Latin into its language. This was the case with Portugal — where the Portuguese language originates — as well as with places like France, Spain, and even Romania.

So how did Portuguese get all the way to Brazil? A Portuguese conquistador named Pedro Álvares Cabral landed in modern-day Brazil on April 22, 1500, and is the person credited for having "discovered" Brazil. Many indigenous people were already living in the area, of course, many of whom spoke a language that's part of a language family today called **Tupi-Guarani** (too-*pee* gwah-dah-*nee*).

Brazilian Portuguese uses some Tupi-Guarani words. Mostly the words appear as names of towns in Brazil — for example, **Ubatuba** (*ooh*-bah-*too*-bah) is a pretty beach town in São Paulo state (it's nicknamed **Uba-Chuva** because **chuva** [*shoo*-vah] means *rain* and it rains there a lot!). Tupi-Guarani words also name native plants and animals. "Armadillo," for example, is **tatu** (tah-*too*). After you get used to speaking Portuguese, telling whether a word is Latin-based or Tupi-Guarani–based is pretty easy.

Still other words in Brazilian Portuguese are based on African languages, from the vast influence that African slaves had on creating modern-day Brazil and its culture.

What you may not realize is that the English language has a lot of Latin influence. Linguists consider English to be a Germanic language, and it technically is. But due to the on-and-off French occupations of the British Isles, some of those French (Latin-based) words rubbed off on English. Some people say as much as 40 percent of English is Latin-based.

That's great news for you. It means many Portuguese words have the same root as English words. The *root* of a word is usually the middle of the word — those few sounds that really define what the word means. Some examples of Portuguese words that resemble English include **experimento** (eh-speh-dee-*men*-toh; experiment), **presidente** (pdeh-zee-*dang*-chee; president), **economia** (eh-koh-noh-*mee*-ah; economy), **decisão** (ah deh-see-*zah*-ooh; decision), **computador** (kom-*poo*-tah-*doh;* computer), **liberdade** (lee-beh-*dah*-jee; liberty), and **banana** (bah-*nah*-nah). And that's only to name a few!

Another benefit: **O português** (ooh poh-too-*gehz;* Portuguese), like all Latin languages, uses the English alphabet. Some funny accent marks appear on some of the vowels, but they just add to the mystique of Portuguese. Learning Portuguese isn't the same as learning Japanese or Arabic, which use totally different alphabets.

Finally, due to the influence the United States has had on the world recently — in some ways greater than Rome's ancient influence — many English words are used commonly in Portuguese, with no adaptation in the way they're written. These words include modern-technology words like **e-mail** (ee-*may*-oh) and also basic words like **shopping** (*shoh*-ping) or **show** (shoh; show/performance).

Reciting Your ABCs

Brazilian Portuguese sounds very strange at first. I myself thought it sounded Russian, back when I didn't understand a **palavra** (pah-*lahv*-dah; word)! A few of the sounds are a little hard to imitate, because people don't use them in English. But Brazilians often understand you even if you don't say words perfectly. Many think a foreign **sotaque** (soh-*tah*-kee; accent) is charming, so don't worry about it.

But the way the sounds correspond to the written letters is very systematic in Brazilian Portuguese — more so than in English. After you get used to the way a letter or combination of letters sounds, you get the hang of pronunciations pretty quickly. There are few surprises in **a pronúncia** (ah pdoh-*noon*-see-ah; pronunciation) after you get the basics down.

At the beginning of this chapter, did you notice how the pronunciation is shown in parentheses after the Portuguese word? That's how this book shows the pronunciation of all new words. The italicized part is where you put the emphasis on the word. In "Words to Know" lists, the part you emphasize is underlined rather than italicized.

Are you ready to learn the basics of **português?** You can start with the alphabet. Practice spelling out your name:

- **a** (ah)
- **b** (beh)
- **c** (seh)
- **d** (deh)
- **e** (eh)
- **f** (*eh*-fee)
- **g** (zheh)
- **h** (ah-*gah*)
- **i** (ee)

- **j** (*zhoh*-tah)
- **k** (kah)
- **l** (*eh*-lee)
- **m** (*eh*-mee)
- **n** (*eh*-nee)
- **o** (awe)
- **p** (peh)
- **q** (keh)
- **r** (*eh*-hee)
- **s** (*eh*-see)
- **t** (teh)
- **u** (ooh)
- **v** (veh)
- **w** (*dah*-blee-ooh)
- **x** (sheez)
- **y** (*eep*-see-long)
- **z** (zeh)

When the book uses the sound *zh* as part of the phonetic transcription (the pronunciation guide in parentheses), think of the sound in Hungarian actress Zsa-Zsa Gabor's name. That's the *zh* sound I'm talking about.

Conquering Consonants

Getting through this book will be a cinch after you go through the basic pronunciation guide in this section. Skipping the guide is okay, too — you can get the gist by reading aloud the pronunciations of words in other chapters. But if you want to get a general idea of how to pronounce words that don't show up in this book, this is a great place to begin. I start with the consonants first — you know, all those letters in the alphabet that aren't vowels.

The most hilarious aspect of Brazilian Portuguese pronunciation occurs when a word ends in a consonant. In most cases, these are foreign (and mostly English) words that Brazilians have adopted. They add an *ee* sound to the end of the word when there isn't one. Here are some examples: **club** (*kloo*-bee); **laptop** (lahp-ee-*top*-ee); **hip-hop** (heep-ee-*hoh*-pee); **rap** (*hah*-pee); and **rock** (*hoh*-kee).

Most consonants in Brazilian Portuguese have the same sound as in English. In the following sections, I go over the exceptions.

The letter C

A *c* that begins a word sounds usually like a *k*.

⮕ **casa** (*kah*-zah; house)

⮕ **café** (kah-*feh;* coffee)

If the *c* has a hook-shaped mark under it, like this — *ç* — it makes an *s* sound.

⮕ **serviço** (seh-*vee*-soo; service)

⮕ **França** (*fdahn*-sah; France)

The most common appearance of what Brazilians call the **c-cedilha** (*seh* seh-*deel*-yah; ç/cedilla) is at the end of a word, followed by **-ão.** It's the Brazilian equivalent of the English *–tion* ending.

⮕ **promoção** (pdoh-moh-*sah*-ooh; sale/discount/sales promotion)

⮕ **evolução** (eh-voh-loo-*sah*-ooh; evolution)

The letter D

If the word begins with a *d,* the sound is usually a hard *d,* like in English.

⮕ **dançar** (dahn-*sah;* to dance)

⮕ **data** (*dah*-tah; date)

The word **de** (jee), which means *of,* is an exception.

If the *d* comes in the middle of a word, before a vowel, it can have either a hard *d* sound or a *j* sound — like in the English word *jelly.*

- ✔ **modelo** (moh-*deh*-loh; model)
- ✔ **estado** (eh-*stah*-doh; state)
- ✔ **advogado** (ahj-voh-*gah*-doh; lawyer)
- ✔ **pedir** (peh-*jee;* to ask for)
- ✔ **liberdade** (lee-beh-*dah*-jee; freedom)

The letter G

The *g* in Portuguese usually is a hard *g,* like in the English word *go.*

- ✔ **gato** (*gah*-toh; cat)
- ✔ **governo** (goh-*veh*-noh; government)
- ✔ **segundo** (seh-*goon*-doh; second)

But it takes a *zh* sound, as in the famous Zsa-Zsa Gabor, when followed by an *e* or an *i.*

- ✔ **gente** (*zhang*-chee; people)
- ✔ **biologia** (bee-oh-loh-*zhee*-ah; biology)

The letter H

The Brazilian Portuguese *h* is one of the most versa-tile consonants around. If the word begins with an *h,* the letter is silent.

- ✔ **honesto** (oh-*neh*-stoh; honest)
- ✔ **hora** (*oh*-dah; hour)

If the *h* follows an *l (lh)* or an *n (nh),* the *h* sounds like a *y.*

- ✔ **maravilhoso** (mah-dah-veel-*yoh*-zoo; marvellous/amazing)
- ✔ **palhaço** (pahl-*yah*-soh; clown)
- ✔ **companhia** (kohm-pahn-*yee*-ah; company)
- ✔ **Espanha** (eh-*spahn*-yah; Spain)

The letter J

The *j* in Portuguese sounds like the *zh* in Zsa-Zsa.

- ✔ **julho** (*zhool*-yoh; July)
- ✔ **Jorge** (*zhoh*-zhee; George)
- ✔ **loja** (*loh*-zhah; store)
- ✔ **joelho** (zhoh-*el*-yoh; knee)

The letter L

The *l* in Portuguese normally sounds like the *l* in English.

- ✔ **líder** (*lee*-deh; leader)
- ✔ **gelo** (*zheh*-loo; ice)

But if it comes at the end of a word, the *l* sounds like *ooh*.

- ✔ **mil** (mee-*ooh;* one thousand)
- ✔ **Natal** (nah-*tah*-ooh; Christmas)

The letters M and N

The *m* and *n* in Portuguese generally sound like *m* and *n* in English.

- ✔ **mel** (*meh*-ooh; honey)
- ✔ **medo** (*meh*-doo; fear)
- ✔ **janela** (zhah-*neh*-lah; window)
- ✔ **não** (*nah*-ooh; no)

But at the end of a word, an *m* or *n* takes on an *ng* sound.

> ✔ **homem** (*oh*-mang; man)
> ✔ **cem** (sang; one hundred)

The letter Q

The *q* in Portuguese has a *k* sound.

> ✔ **quilo** (kee-*loo;* kilo)
> ✔ **quilômetro** (kee-*loh*-meh-tdoh; kilometer)

The letter R

If the word begins or ends with an *r,* the *r* sounds like an *h.*

> ✔ **Roberto** (hoh-*beh*-too; Robert)
> ✔ **rosa** (*hoh*-zah; pink)

If the *r* comes in the middle of a word, on the accented syllable, it sounds like an even stronger *h.* In the words **porta** and **carta** that follow, push air out of your mouth as you say the *h.* It's a breathy *h,* not a guttural sound like you'd hear in Hebrew or German.

> ✔ **porta** (*poh*-tah; door)
> ✔ **carta** (*kah*-tah; letter)

If the *r* comes in the middle of a word, on an unaccented syllable, it sounds like a soft *d.* Feel what your mouth does when you read the pronunciation for **Brasil.** The way you say the *d* in *bdah* is how you should say it in the *dah* of koh-dah-*sah*-ooh, too. It's not a hard *d* like in English.

> ✔ **Brasil** (bdah-*zeeh*-ooh; Brazil)
> ✔ **coração** (koh-dah-*sah*-ooh; heart)

If a word has two *rs (rr),* they make an *h* sound, as in **burro** (*boo*-hoh; dumb).

If the *r* comes at the end of a word, it's silent.

> ✔ **caminhar** (kah-ming-*yah;* to walk)
>
> ✔ **gostar** (goh-*stah;* to like)

The letter S

The *s* is the same as the English *s,* except it becomes a *z* sound at the end of a word.

> ✔ **olhos** (*ohl*-yooz; eyes)
>
> ✔ **dedos** (*deh*-dooz; fingers)

The letter T

The *t* in Portuguese has a soft *t* sound in general. In English, you don't use the soft *t* sound very often. Say *ta, ta, ta* in a quiet voice, as if you're marking a rhythm. That's the soft *t* of Portuguese.

> ✔ **motocicleta** (moh-too-see-*kleh*-tah; motorcycle)
>
> ✔ **atuar** (ah-too-*ah;* to act)
>
> ✔ **Tailândia** (tah-ee-*lahn*-jee-ah; Thailand)

But *t* sounds like *ch* when followed by an *e* or an *i.*

> ✔ **passaporte** (pah-sah-*poh*-chee; passport)
>
> ✔ **forte** (*foh*-chee; strong)
>
> ✔ **notícia** (noh-*chee*-see-ah; news)
>
> ✔ **time** (*chee*-mee; team)

The letter W

The *w* doesn't naturally occur in Portuguese, but when it does, it sounds like a *v.* The only places you really see a *w* is in someone's name.

> ✔ **Wanderlei** (*vahn*-deh-lay)
>
> ✔ **Wanessa** (vah-*neh*-sah)

The letter X

The *x* generally has a *sh* sound in Portuguese.

- ✔ **axé** (ah-*sheh;* a popular Brazilian type of dance)
- ✔ **lixo** (*lee*-shoo; garbage)
- ✔ **taxa** (*tah*-shah; rate)
- ✔ **bruxa** (*bdoo*-shah; witch)

But it can also have a *ks* sound, like in English: **tóxico** (*tohk*-see-koh; toxic).

Exercising Your Jowls with Vowels

In this section, I go over all five vowels in Portuguese, including the ones with the weird accents on top of them.

The letters A and Ã

The *a* normally has an *ah* sound.

- ✔ **amigo** (ah-*mee*-goo; friend)
- ✔ **ajuda** (ah-*zhoo*-dah; help)
- ✔ **Tatiana** (tah-chee-*ah*-nah)

If the *a* has a squiggly mark, or **til** (*chee*-ooh; ~/tilde*)*, on top of it (*ã*), the letter makes a nasal sound. Instead of opening your mouth to say *a,* as in the English word *at,* try closing your mouth almost completely while you make the same sound. Do you hear that? It becomes more of an *uh* than an *ah.* Then try to open your mouth (making the same sound) without bringing your lips farther apart. And voilá! You have the *ã* sound!

The *ã* is a very common sound in Brazilian Portuguese. But to be honest, I took more than a year to be able to say it like a Brazilian. Don't sweat it — most Brazilians will probably understand you either way.

The *ã* occasionally comes at the end of a word.

> ✔ **maçã** (mah-*sah;* apple)
>
> ✔ **Maracanã** (mah-dah-kah-*nah;* a soccer stadium in Rio)

However, *ã* is usually followed by an *o (ão)*. Together, these letters make an *ah-ooh* sound. But say it fast, and you say *Ow!* like you've hurt yourself. Brazilians say the *ã* like the English *ow,* only with the nasal sound you just practiced.

> ✔ **não** (*nah*-ooh; no)
>
> ✔ **informação** (een-foh-mah-*sah*-ooh; information)

The letters E and Ê

In general, the *e* sounds like *eh,* as in *egg* or *ten.*

> ✔ **elefante** (eh-leh-*fahn*-chee; elephant)
>
> ✔ **dedo** (*deh*-doo; finger)

If it comes at the end of a word, though, *e* usually has an *ee* sound.

> ✔ **dificuldade** (jee-fee-kool-*dah*-jee; difficulty)
>
> ✔ **boate** (boh-*ah*-chee; nightclub)

If the *e* has a hat on it *(ê)*, don't worry. It has the same *eh* sound as normal.

> ✔ **três** (tdehz; three)

The letter I

The *i* has an *ee* sound, pretty much without exception.

> ✔ **inglês** (eeng-*glehz;* English)
>
> ✔ **livro** (*leev*-doh; book)

The letters O and Ô

The *o* by itself has an easy-to-make *oh* sound.

  ✔ **ontem** (*ohn*-tang; yesterday)

  ✔ **onda** (*ohn*-dah; wave)

At the end of a word, though, it usually sounds like *ooh*.

  ✔ **tudo** (*too*-doo; everything/all)

  ✔ **Gramado** (gdah-*mah*-doo; a city in Rio Grande do Sul, famous for its film festival)

The *o* also comes with a hat on it *(ô)*. Don't fear the weirdness — it takes an *oh* sound, like normal.

  ✔ **ônibus** (*oh*-nee-boos; bus)

The letter U

The *u* has an *ooh* sound.

  ✔ **urso** (*ooh*-soo; bear)

  ✔ **útil** (*ooh*-chee-ooh; useful)

  ✔ **ou** (oh; or)

Chapter 2

Grammar on a Diet: Just the Basics

- -

In This Chapter

▶ Forming simple sentences

▶ Understanding regular and irregular verb conjugations

▶ Making connections

▶ Cluing in on contractions

▶ Indirect objects: When something happens to you and me

▶ Stating possessives

- -

*I*ck. Grammar. Remember that word from high school? The way grammar is usually taught, you feel like you're doing math problems, not exploring fun cultural stuff. Well, in this chapter, I don't talk about grammar as a set of rules to memorize. Think of this as grammar made fun.

Constructing Simple Sentences

A simple sentence construction (in French or in English) consists of a noun, an adjective, a verb, and, possibly, an adverb.

Nouns

As in English, nouns are one of the main parts of Portuguese speech — the most important pieces of the puzzle. They're used to name people, places, and things, like **casa** (*kah*-zah; house), **amigo** (ah-*mee*-goo; friend), **Maria** (mah-*dee*-ah; the name of a woman), **caneta** (kah-*neh*-tah; pen), and **Brasil** (bdah-*zee*-ooh; Brazil).

Portuguese nouns come in two types: masculine and feminine. Masculine nouns usually end in *–o,* and feminine nouns usually end in *–a.*

Adjectives

Keeping the gender of the thing you're talking about in mind is important because every time you describe the noun with an adjective — like **bonita** (boo-*nee*-tah; pretty), **simpático** (seem-*pah*-chee-koo; nice), or **grande** (*gdahn*-jee; big) — you change the end of the adjective to match the gender of the noun. Like nouns, masculine adjectives normally end in *–o,* and feminine adjectives end in *–a.*

In Portuguese, the adjective normally comes *after* the noun.

Here's how the nouns and adjectives get paired off:

- ✔ **homem lindo** (*oh*-mang *leen*-doo; good-looking/handsome man)
- ✔ **mulher linda** (mool-*yeh* *leen*-dah; good-looking/beautiful woman)
- ✔ **quarto limpo** (*kwah*-too *leem*-poo; clean room)
- ✔ **casa suja** (*kah*-zah *soo*-zhah; dirty house)
- ✔ **comida gostosa** (koh-*mee*-dah goh-*stoh*-zah; delicious food)

Some adjectives are neutral and stay the same for both masculine and feminine nouns. These adjectives often end in *–e* rather than *–o* or *–a.* Adjectives in this group include **inteligente** (een-*teh*-lee-*zhang*-chee; intelligent) and **grande** (*gdahn*-jee; big).

Notice how the word **inteligente** stays the same, whether the noun is male or female:

> ✔ **Ela é muito inteligente.** (*eh*-lah *eh* moh-*ee*-toh een-*teh*-lee-*zhang*-chee; She is very intelligent.)

> ✔ **Ele é muito inteligente.** (*eh*-lee *eh* moh-*ee*-toh een-*teh*-lee-*zhang*-chee; He is very intelligent.)

If the noun is plural, just add an *s* to the end of the adjective: **cachorros pequenos** (kah-*shoh*-hooz peh-*keh*-nooz; small dogs).

Articles

Just as with Portuguese nouns and adjectives, the gender game is also at play when it comes to articles — words like *the, a, an,* and *some*.

Now's the time to *ooh* and *ah* over grammar — **o** (ooh) means "the" for masculine nouns, and **a** (ah) means "the" for feminine nouns:

> ✔ **o homem lindo** (ooh *oh*-mang *leen*-doo; the handsome man)

> ✔ **a mulher linda** (ah mool-*yeh leen*-dah; the beautiful woman)

> ✔ **o quarto limpo** (ooh *kwah*-too *leem*-poo; the clean room)

> ✔ **a casa suja** (ah *kah*-zah *soo*-zhah; the dirty house)

If a noun is plural, use **os** (ooz) if the noun's masculine and **as** (ahz) if it's feminine:

> ✔ **os barcos grandes** (ooz *bah*-kooz *gdahn*-jeez; the big boats)

> ✔ **as flores amarelas** (ahz *floh*-deez ah-mah-*deh*-lahz; the yellow flowers)

Brazilians use the word *the* in front of nouns much more often than people do in English. When you'd say, "Books are fun," they'd say **Os livros são divertidos** (oohz *leev*-dooz *sah*-ooh jee-veh-*chee*-dooz; *Literally:* The books are fun). "Brazil is big" would be **O Brasil é grande** (ooh bdah-*zee*-ooh eh *gdahn*-jee; *Literally:* The Brazil is big).

To say "a," as in "a hat" or "a table," say **um** (oong) for masculine nouns and **uma** (*ooh*-mah) for feminine nouns:

- ✔ **um banheiro** (oong bahn-*yay*-doh; a bathroom)
- ✔ **uma pessoa** (*ooh*-mah peh-*soh*-ah; a person)
- ✔ **um livro** (oong *leev*-doh; a book)
- ✔ **uma mesa** (*ooh*-mah *meh*-zah; a table)

To say "some," use **uns** (oonz) if the noun is masculine or **umas** (*ooh*-mahz) if it's feminine:

- ✔ **uns sapatos** (*oonz* sah-*pah*-tooz; some shoes)
- ✔ **umas garotas** (*ooh*-mahz gah-*doh*-tahz; some girls)
- ✔ **umas praias** (*ooh*-mahz *pdah*-ee-ahz; some beaches)

When you make the plural of a word ending in *–m,* such as **um,** the *m* always changes to an *n:* **Um homem** (*oong oh*-mang; a man) becomes **uns homens** (*oonz oh*-mangz; the men).

Pronouns

You use pronouns to refer to people when you don't say their names. Here's the way Brazilians do it:

- ✔ **eu** (*eh*-ooh; I)
- ✔ **você** (voh-*seh;* you)
- ✔ **ele** (*eh*-lee; he/him)
- ✔ **ela** (*eh*-lah; she/her)

- ✔ **nós** (nohz; we/us)
- ✔ **eles** (*eh*-leez; they/them — all males or males and females)
- ✔ **elas** (*eh*-lahz; they/them — all females)

Brazilians don't have an equivalent of the English word *it*. Because "things" are either masculine or feminine in Portuguese, Brazilians refer to the thing or things as **ele/ela/eles/elas** when the thing isn't named.

If you're talking to a person who's a lot older than you (especially the elderly) or to an important person like a boss or a politician, instead of using **você**, use **o senhor** (ooh seen-*yoh; Literally:* the gentleman) or **a senhora** (ah seen-*yoh*-dah; *Literally:* the lady) to show respect.

Verbs

To really make a sentence come alive, you need verbs. Along with nouns, verbs make up the main parts of a sentence. Verbs can link a describing word to what it describes. The most basic linking-verb words in Portuguese are **é** (eh; is) and **são** (*sah*-ooh; are). The following sentences simply use nouns, verbs, and adjectives in the same order you'd use them in English:

- ✔ **A casa é bonita.** (ah *kah*-zah *eh* boo-*nee*-tah; The house is pretty.)
- ✔ **O amigo é simpático.** (ooh ah-*mee*-goo *eh* seem-*pah*-chee-koo; The friend is nice.)
- ✔ **As rosas são vermelhas.** (ahz *hoh*-zahz *sah*-ooh veh-*mel*-yahz; The roses are red.)

Of course, all you need to create a sentence is a noun followed by a verb. When the person, place, or thing is doing something, a verb signals the action. Action verbs include **estuda** (eh-*stoo*-dah; studies), **vai** (*vah*-ee; goes), and **canta** (*kahn*-tah; sings). Here are some complete sentences:

✔ **Os amigos falam.** (oohz ah-*mee*-gooz *fah*-lah-ooh; The friends talk.)

✔ **O gato dorme.** (ooh *gah*-too *doh*-mee; The cat sleeps.)

✔ **A mãe cozinha.** (ah *mah*-ee koh-*zing*-yah; The mom cooks.)

When you want to ask a question, you don't have to change the order of the words. Just say the same thing, but raise the pitch of your voice at the end of the sentence. Use the voice you use to ask questions in English; it's that easy.

✔ **A casa é bonita?** (ah *kah*-zah *eh* boo-*nee*-tah; Is the house pretty?)

✔ **As rosas são vermelhas?** (ahz *hoh*-zahz *sah*-ooh veh-*mel*-yahz; Are the roses red?)

The verb can change a bit depending on who's doing the action. The next section tells you how to know which verb form to use.

The Simple Tenses: Present, Past, and Future

Tense simply means "time." So if you want to express an action or a state of being taking place in the present, you use the present tense. If it hasn't happened yet, you use the future tense. And if it took place in the past, you use the past tense.

For each tense, you have to conjugate the verb. *Conjugation* is basically a matter of matching a verb to a subject. Portuguese verbs come in three varieties: those that end in –ar, –er, and –ir. The –ar ending is your best friend; with a few exceptions, –ar verbs tend to be conjugated the same way, all the time. The –ir and –er verbs can be a little trickier. There are general rules for their conjugation, but not all verbs ending in –ir or –er follow the rules.

To conjugate a verb, you snip off the ending (–ar, –er, –ir) and add a new one, depending on who's doing the action. The following sections explain which endings to use.

In this book, I separate **você** (you) and **ele/ela** (him/her) into different lines even though they use the same conjugation. I also don't show in the conjugation charts the formal version of *you:* **o senhor/a senhora** (ooh seen-*yoh*/ah seen-*yoh*-dah). This form of address uses the same conjugation as **você** and **ele/ela.** So whenever you want to say *you* — whether you're being formal or not — you can always use the same form of the verb.

If the noun is not a person but rather a thing or place, first check out whether it's singular or plural. If it's singular, use the **ele/ela** conjugation; if it's plural, use the **eles/elas** conjugation.

Sometimes, you don't have to conjugate the verb at all. This often happens when you'd use an -*ing* ending in English: **Dançar é divertido** (dahn-*sah eh* jee-veh-*chee*-doo; Dancing is fun). **Falar português não é difícil** (fah-*lah* poh-too-*gez nah*-ooh *eh* jee-*fee*-see-ooh; Speaking Portuguese is not hard).

Present tense

To use a verb that ends in –ar, replace the –ar with one of the new verb endings: –o, –a, –a, –amos, and –am; which ending you choose depends on the subject of the sentence. Table 2-1 shows you how the endings match up with the pronouns.

Table 2-1	Verb Endings to Use with –ar Verbs
Portuguese Pronoun	*Verb Ending*
eu	–o
você	–a
ele/ela	–a
nós	–amos
eles/elas	–am

Conjugating regular –er and –ir verbs isn't difficult.
For most –er and –ir verbs, just replace the –er or –ir
with –o, –e, –e, –emos/–imos, or –em. Table 2-2 shows
you which endings to use.

Table 2-2	Verb Endings to Use with Regular –er and –ir Verbs
Portuguese Pronoun	*Verb Ending*
eu	–o
você	–e
ele/ela	–e
nós	-emos (for –er verbs), –imos (for –ir verbs)
eles/elas	–em

Many –er and –ir verbs have special endings. With
verbs that end in –zer, for example, like **fazer** (fah-*zeh;*
to do) and **trazer** (tdah-*zeh;* to bring), you remove
–zer to get the stem; the verbs then take the following
endings: –ço, –z, –z, –zemos, and –zem. The last two

endings are similar to the –er verb endings (for *we* and *they*), but the first few endings (for *I* and *you/he/she*) are indeed bizarre. Here are some examples, using the *I* and *you* forms:

- ✔ **Eu faço muitas coisas.** (*eh*-ooh *fah*-soo moh-*ee*-tahz *koy*-zahz; I do many things.)

- ✔ **Você traz um presente.** (voh-*seh tdah*-eez oong pdeh-*zang*-chee; You bring a present.)

Past tense

Not everything happens in the **aqui** (ah-*kee;* here) and **agora** (ah-*goh*-dah; now). To say stuff that happened in the **passado** (pah-*sah*-doh; past), you need to change the verb conjugation.

For –ar verbs, the past-tense conjugations go like this. Take off the –ar from the verb, and add on the endings shown in Table 2-3.

Table 2-3	Verb Endings to Use with Regular –ar Verbs
Subject Pronoun	*Past-Tense Verb Ending*
eu	–ei
você	–ou
ele/ela	–ou
nós	–amos (same as in present tense)
eles/elas	–aram

For –er and –ir verbs, the past tense conjugations go like what you see in Table 2-4.

Table 2-4	Verb Endings to Use with Regular –er and –ir Verbs
Subject Pronoun	*Past-Tense Verb Ending*
eu	–i
você	–eu
ele/ela	–eu
nós	–emos (for –er verbs), –imos (for –ir verbs) [same as in present tense]
eles/elas	–eram (for –er verbs), –iram (for –ir verbs)

Future tense

To talk about events in the future, all you have to do is conjugate **ir** (eeh; to go/to be going), add another verb, and voilá: *You're going to. . . , He's going to. . . , We're going to. . . .* For example, **Nós vamos dançar** (*nohz* vah-mohz dahn-*sah*) means "We're going to dance."

First take a look at the present tense (the here and now) conjugations for **ir:**

Conjugation	*Pronunciation*
eu vou	*eh*-ooh *voh*
você vai	voh-*seh vah*-ee
ele/ela vai	*eh*-lee/*eh*-lah *vah*-ee
nós vamos	nohz *vah*-mohz
eles/elas vão	*eh*-leez/*eh*-lahz *vah*-ooh

Try the magic first with the verb **viajar** (vee-ah-*zhah*; to travel/to take a trip):

Conjugation	Pronunciation
eu vou viajar	*eh*-ooh *voh* vee-ah-*zhah*
você vai viajar	voh-*seh vah*-ee vee-ah-*zhah*
ele/ela vai viajar	*eh*-lee/*eh*-lah *vah*-ee vee-ah-*zhah*
nós vamos viajar	*nohz* vah-mohz vee-ah-*zhah*
eles/elas vão viajar	*eh*-leez/*eh*-lahz *vah*-ooh vee-ah-*zhah*

Brazilians like to say *who's* going to do something except when they're talking about **nós** (nohz; we) and **eu** (*eh*-ooh; I). They often leave out the **nós** or the **eu** and just start the sentence with the verb, **vamos** or **vou**.

Conjugating the tenses

Tables 2-5 through 2-11 show you how to conjugate all three tenses of several common verbs.

All regular verbs conjugate the same way, so you can flip back to this section when you want to know how to conjugate a new regular verb.

Table 2-5	Regular –ar Verb Morar (To Live)		
	Present	*Past*	*Future*
eu (I)	moro	morei	vou morar
você (you)	mora	morou	vai morar
ele/ela (he/she)	mora	morou	vai morar
nós (we)	moramos	moramos	vamos morar
eles/elas (they)	moram	moraram	vão morar

Table 2-6	Regular –er Verb Comer (To Eat)		
	Present	*Past*	*Future*
eu (I)	como	comi	vou comer
você (you)	come	comeu	vai comer
ele/ela (he/she)	come	comeu	vai comer
nós (we)	comemos	comemos	vamos comer
eles/elas (they)	comem	comeram	vão comer

Table 2-7	Regular –ir Verb Abrir (To Open)		
	Present	*Past*	*Future*
eu (I)	abro	abri	vou abrir
você (you)	abre	abriu	vai abrir
ele/ela (he/she)	abre	abriu	vai abrir
nós (we)	abrimos	abrimos	vamos abrir
eles/elas (they)	abrem	abriram	vão abrir

Table 2-8	Irregular Estar (To Be Temporarily)		
	Present	*Past*	*Future*
eu	estou	estive	vou estar
você	está	esteve	vai estar
ele/ela	está	esteve	vai estar
nós	estamos	estivemos	vamos estar
eles/elas	estão	estiveram	vão estar

Table 2-9	Irregular Verb Ir (To Go)		
	Present	*Past*	*Future*
eu	vou	fui	vou ir
você	vai	foi	vai ir
ele/ela	vai	foi	vai ir
nós	vamos	fomos	vamos ir
eles/elas	vão	foram	vão ir

Table 2-10	Irregular Verb Ser (To Be Permanently)		
	Present	*Past*	*Future*
eu	sou	fui	vou ser
você	é	foi	vai ser
ele/ela	é	foi	vai ser
nós	somos	fomos	vamos ser
eles/elas	são	foram	vão ser

Table 2-11	Irregular Verb Ter (To Have)		
	Present	*Past*	*Future*
eu	tenho	tive	vou ter
você	tem	teve	vai ter
ele/ela	tem	teve	vai ter
nós	temos	tivemos	vamos ter
eles/elas	têm	tiveram	vão ter

Connecting It All Together

The little connector words in Table 2-12 make the rest of the sentence fit together and help you sound like a native.

Table 2-12	Connector Words: Conjunctions and Prepositions	
Term	**Pronunciation**	**Meaning**
e	ee	and
além de	ah-*lang* jee	in addition to
mas	*mah*-eez	but
para	*pah*-dah	to/in order to
se	see	if
mesmo se	*mehz*-moh see	even if
embora	ehm-*boh*-dah	although
que	kee	that
só que	*soh* kee	except that
desde	*dehz*-jee	since
porque	poh-*keh*	because
até	ah-*teh*	until
com	*koh*-oong	with
por	poh	through/by
de	jee	of
sobre	*soh*-bdee	about/on top of

Here are a few examples of connectors in sentences:

- ✔ **Romeu e Julieta** (hoh-*meh*-ooh ee zhoo-lee-*eh*-tah; Romeo and Juliet)

- ✔ **café com leite** (kah-*feh* koh-oong *lay*-chee; coffee with milk)

- ✔ **desde a primeira vez que eu te vi** (*dehz*-jee ah pdee-*may*-dah *vehz* kee *eh*-ooh chee *vee;* ever since I first saw you)

- ✔ **é para você** (eh *pah*-dah voh-*seh;* it's for you)

Making Contractions: It's a Cinch!

When you make contractions in English — in words like *can't* and *don't* — you use an apostrophe to show that a letter is missing. Brazilians likewise combine words so they're shorter or easier to pronounce, but Portuguese doesn't use apostrophes.

Take a look at what happens in Portuguese when you combine **em** and **o. Em** (ang) means "in/on," and **o** (oh) means "the." But **em o** (in the) doesn't exist in Portuguese, because Brazilians use the contraction **no** (noo):

- ✔ **no banheiro** (noo bahn-*yay*-doh; in the bathroom)

- ✔ **no quarto** (noo *kwah*-too; in the room)

- ✔ **no teto** (noo *teh*-too; on the roof)

The previous examples are for singular, masculine nouns. Take a look at what happens with feminine and plural nouns. Instead of **no,** you now have **na** (feminine and singular), **nos** (masculine and plural), and **nas** (feminine and plural):

- ✔ **na mesa** (nah *meh*-zah; on the table)

- ✔ **na cozinha** (nah koh-*zing*-yah; in the kitchen)

- ✔ **na rua** (nah *hoo*-ah; on the street)

✔ **nos livros** (nooz *leev*-dooz; in books)

✔ **nas praias** (nahz *pdah*-ee-ahz; on beaches)

Contractions with **o** also happen with **de** (deh; of) and **por** (poh; through/on/around). For example, when you want to say "of the," you combine **de** and **o** to form **do/da/dos/das.** To say "through/on/around the," use **pelo/pela/pelos/pelas.** (If you're confused about which form to use, just remember that *o* goes with masculine nouns, *a* goes with feminine, and *s* makes words plural.)

Here are some examples:

✔ **do computador** (doo kom-*poo*-tah-*doh;* of the computer)

✔ **das professoras** (dahz pdoh-feh-*soh*-dahz; of the teachers)

✔ **pelo telefone** (*peh*-loo teh-leh-*foh*-nee; on the phone)

✔ **pelas ruas** (*peh*-lahz *hooh*-ahz; through the streets)

✔ **dos pais** (dooz *pah*-eez; of the parents)

To Me, to You: Indirect Objects

One of my favorite aspects of Portuguese grammar is the way they talk about *me* and *you* being on the receiving end. In grammar books, these words are called *indirect objects;* the words *me* and *you* are in the sentence, but they're not the ones doing the action.

Te (teh) means "you," and **me** (meh) means "me" (that one's easy to remember). Put these indirect objects right before the verb. Take a look at some examples:

✔ **Eu te dou dinheiro.** (*eh*-ooh chee *doh* jing-*yay*-doh; I give you money.)

✔ **Me diga o seu nome.** (mee *jee*-gah ooh *seh*-ooh *noh*-mee; Tell me your name.)

In the first sentence, **eu** is the subject. In the second sentence, the subject isn't even stated. You can tell that the verb **diga** is in the **você/ele/ela** form.

Commanding an Audience

Just as in English, you can drop the *you* at the beginning of a sentence when you're telling someone to do something. Brazilians love to use the formula **Me** plus a verb:

- ✔ **Me faz um recibo, por favor?** (mee *fah*-eez oong heh-*see*-boo poh fah-*voh;* Can you write a receipt for me, please?)

- ✔ **Me traz uma água, por favor.** (mee *tdah*-eez ooh-mah *ah*-gwah, poh fah-*voh;* Bring me a water, please.)

- ✔ **Me explica o que aconteceu.** (mee eh-*splee*-kah ooh *kee* ah-kohn-teh-*seh*-ooh; Explain to me what happened.)

- ✔ **Me leva até a rodoviária?** (mee *leh*-vah ah-*teh* ah hoh-doh-vee-*ah*-dee-ah; Can you take me to the bus station?)

- ✔ **Me dá o seu passaporte, por favor.** (mee *dah* ooh seh-ooh pah-sah-*poh*-chee poh fah-*voh;* Give me your passport, please.)

Getting Possessive

If you want to express "It's mine," say **É meu** (eh *meh*-ooh) while you're pointing to something. To say "It's yours," use the phrase **É seu** (*eh seh*-ooh). To say "It's ours," use the phrase **É nosso** (*eh noh*-soo). If you want to specify what exactly is yours, change the **meu, seu,** or **nosso** to match the thing that you're talking about. Just ask yourself: Is the name of that thing a masculine or feminine word? Is it singular or plural? Check out Table 2-13 for the possibilities of combinations for talking about "my" things, "your" things, and "our" things.

Table 2-13   Possessive Words — My, Your, and Our

Meaning	Singular Masculine	Singular Feminine	Plural Masculine	Plural Feminine
my	o meu (*ooh meh-ooh*)	a minha (*ah ming-yah*)	os meus (*ooz meh-ooz*)	as minhas (*ahz ming-yahz*)
your	o seu (*ooh seh-ooh*)	a sua (*ah soo-ah*)	os seus (*ooz seh-ooz*)	as suas (*ahz soo-ahz*)
our	o nosso (*ooh noh-soo*)	a nossa (*ah noh-sah*)	os nossos (*ooz noh-sooz*)	as nossas (*ahz noh-sahz*)

Take a look at some examples that may come up in a **hotel** (oh-*tay*-ooh; hotel) or **pousada** (poh-*zah*-dah; guesthouse):

- ✔ **o meu passaporte** (ooh *meh*-ooh pah-sah-*poh*-chee; my passport)
- ✔ **o seu cartão de crédito** (ooh *seh*-ooh kah-*tah*-ooh jee *kdeh*-jee-toh; your credit card)
- ✔ **as nossas bagagens** (ahz *noh*-sahz bah-*gah*-zhangz; our baggage)
- ✔ **os nossos planos** (ooz *noh*-sooz *plah*-nohz; our plans)

When you want to talk about "his," "her," or "their" things, you have to switch the word order. Instead of putting the possessive word in *front* of the thing (**o meu quarto** [ooh *meh*-ooh *kwah*-too; my room]), first say what the thing is, and then say **de** (deh; of) plus the owner. The **de** gets attached to the **ele, ela,** or **eles/elas** (the "him," "her," or "them"), and the **e** between the words is dropped.

- ✔ **dele** (*deh*-lee; his. *Literally:* of him)

- ✔ **dela** (*deh*-lah; her. *Literally:* of her)

- ✔ **deles** (*deh*-leez; their — for all males or males and females. *Literally:* of them)

- ✔ **delas** (*deh*-lahz; their — for all females. *Literally:* of them)

Technically, when you say **o quarto dele** (ooh *kwah*-toh *deh*-lee; his room), you're saying "the room of him."

Name the thing first, and then say whose it is.

- ✔ **o dinheiro dela** (ooh jing-*yay*-doh *deh*-lah; her money)

- ✔ **a comida deles** (ah koh-*mee*-dah *deh*-leez; their food — for all males or males and females)

- ✔ **as roupas delas** (ahz *hoh*-pahz *deh*-lahz; their clothes — for all females)

Using a specific name is the easiest situation. Just say the name of the thing plus **de** and the specific name. Also note that people's names always take an *o* or an *a* before them (depending on whether the person is male or female); when combined with **de,** these words become **do** or **da.** When you want to say "Lucia's house," you can say **a casa da Lucia** (ah *kah*-zah dah loo-*see*-ah), which literally means "the house of Lucia." Check out some other examples:

- ✔ **o carro do Mario** (ooh *kah*-hoh doo *mah*-dee-oh; Mario's car)

- ✔ **o cabelo da Ana Cristina** (ooh kah-*beh*-loh dah *ah*-nah kdee-*schee*-nah; Ana Cristina's hair)

- ✔ **as empresas da Petrobrás** (ahz ehm-*pdeh*-zahz dah peh-tdoh-*bdah*-eez; Petrobras's companies — Petrobrás is Brazil's largest oil company)

- ✔ **as praias do Pará** (ahz *pdah*-ee-ahz doo pah-*dah;* Para state's beaches)

Chapter 3

Numerical Gumbo:
Counting of All Kinds

. . . .

In This Chapter

▶ Counting to ten

▶ Telling time

▶ Ticking off the calendar

▶ Spending money

. . . .

*G*ood news! Numerals are the same in Portuguese as in English, so inside a Brazilian store, you can understand the price of something — even if you don't remember a word of Portuguese. This may sound obvious, but the point is that a little familiarity in new surroundings can give you the reassurance and courage to have a little chat with the store clerk. This chapter also shows you how to tell time and navigate the calendar.

Numbers to Know: When Everything Counts

Whether you're telling the time, asking about street numbers, or discussing prices, you need to know how to say numbers. Here are numbers one through ten:

▶ **um** (oong; one)

▶ **dois** (*doh*-eez; two)

- ✔ **três** (tdehz; three)
- ✔ **quatro** (*kwah*-tdoo; four)
- ✔ **cinco** (*sing*-koo; five)
- ✔ **seis** (*say*-eez; six)
- ✔ **sete** (*seh*-chee; seven)
- ✔ **oito** (*oh*-ee-toh; eight)
- ✔ **nove** (*noh*-vee; nine)
- ✔ **dez** (dez; ten)

Now check out how to say 11 through 19:

- ✔ **onze** (*ohn*-zee; 11)
- ✔ **doze** (*doh*-zee; 12)
- ✔ **treze** (*tdeh*-zee; 13)
- ✔ **quatorze** (kah-*toh*-zee; 14)
- ✔ **quinze** (*keen*-zee; 15)
- ✔ **dezeseis** (dez-eh-*say*-eez; 16)
- ✔ **dezesete** (dez-eh-*seh*-chee; 17)
- ✔ **dezoito** (dez-*oh*-ee-toh; 18)
- ✔ **dezenove** (dez-eh-*noh*-vee; 19)

And these are numbers 20 to 100, counting by tens:

- ✔ **vinte** (*ving*-chee; 20)
- ✔ **trinta** (*tdeen*-tah; 30)
- ✔ **quarenta** (kwah-*dang*-tah; 40)
- ✔ **cinqüenta** (sing-*kwen*-tah; 50)
- ✔ **sessenta** (seh-*sen*-tah; 60)
- ✔ **setenta** (seh-*ten*-tah; 70)
- ✔ **oitenta** (oh-ee-*ten*-tah; 80)
- ✔ **noventa** (noh-*ven*-tah; 90)
- ✔ **cem** (sang; 100)

To say a double-digit number that doesn't end in zero, you just put the word **e** (ee; and) in between your tens and ones digits. If you want to say *34,* for example, say **trinta e quatro** (*tdeen*-tah ee *kwah*-tdoh; *Literally:* 30 and 4).

To say 101 through 199, use **cento e** (*sehn*-too ee) plus the rest of number: **Cento e trinta e quatro** (*sehn*-too ee *tdeen*-tah ee *kwah*-tdoh) is 134, and **cento e oitenta e sete** (*sehn*-too ee oh-ee-*ten*-tah ee *seh*-chee) is 187.

For 201 through 999, replace the **cento** with the following hundreds terms:

- ✔ **duzentos** (doo-*zen*-tooz; 200)
- ✔ **trezentos** (tdeh-*zen*-tooz; 300)
- ✔ **quatrocentos** (kwah-tdoo-*sen*-tooz; 400)
- ✔ **quinhentos** (keen-*yen*-tooz; 500)
- ✔ **seiscentos** (say-*sen*-tooz; 600)
- ✔ **setecentos** (*seh*-chee-*sen*-tooz; 700)
- ✔ **oitocentos** (*oh*-ee-too-*sen*-tooz; 800)
- ✔ **novecentos** (*noh*-vee-*sen*-tooz; 900)

One thousand is **mil** (*mee*-ooh), and *one million* is **um milhão** (oong meel-*yah*-ooh). For numbers in those ranges, just add an **e** and then the rest of the number.

The Big Countdown: Ordinal Numbers

When people give directions, they often use ordinal numbers. Someone may tell you to take the **primeira** (pdee-*may*-dah; first) left and then the **terceira** (teh-*say*-dah; third) right. Or someone may say to take the elevator to the **sétimo** (*seh*-chee-moh; seventh) floor. Here's a handy list for all that:

- ✔ **primeiro** (pdee-*may*-doh; first)
- ✔ **segundo** (seh-*goon*-doh; second)

✔ **terceiro** (teh-*say*-doh; third)

✔ **quarto** (*kwah*-toh; fourth)

✔ **quinto** (*keen*-toh; fifth)

✔ **sexto** (*sehs*-toh; sixth)

✔ **sétimo** (*seh*-chee-moh; seventh)

✔ **oitavo** (oh-ee-*tah*-voh; eighth)

✔ **nono** (*noh*-noh; ninth)

Try to remember to change the ending to –**a** instead of –**o** if the following word is feminine.

Here are some example sentences using the ordinal numbers:

✔ **Pega a primeira direita.** (*peh*-gah ah pdee-*may*-dah jee-*day*-tah; Take the first right.)

✔ **Moro no quarto andar.** (*moh*-doo noh *kwah*-toh ahn-*dah;* I live on the fourth floor.)

✔ **É a segunda porta.** (*eh* ah seh-*goon*-dah *poh*-tah; It's the second door.)

Telling Time

Saying the time of **dia** (*jee*-ah; day) is easy in Portuguese. With a little practice, you can have it memorized in no time. Just say **São . . .** (the number of hours) **e . . .** (the number of minutes) **horas: São cinco e quinze** (*sah*-ooh *sing*-koh ee *keen*-zee; It's 5:15).

Most of the time, people don't even say the word **horas.** Using the word **horas** is similar to saying *o'clock,* which is optional: **São sete** (*sah*-ooh ahz *seh*-chee; It's seven) and **São sete horas** (*sah*-ooh ahz *seh*-chee *oh*-dahz; It's seven o'clock) both mean the same thing. If it's half past the hour, say **e meia** (ee *may*-ah; and a half). Here are some examples:

✔ **São duas horas.** (*sah*-ooh *doo*-ahz *oh*-dahz; It's two o'clock.)

✔ **São duas e meia.** (*sah*-ooh *doo*-ahz ee *may*-ah; It's 2:30.)

✔ **São quinze para as três.** (*sah*-ooh *keen*-zee pah-dah ahz *tdehz;* It's 15 to 3:00 [2:45].)

✔ **São onze e quinze.** (*sah*-ooh *ohn*-zee ee *keen*-zee; It's 11:15.)

✔ **São oito e dez.** (*sah*-ooh *oh*-ee-toh ee *dez;* It's 8:10.)

In English, people sometimes give the time as "quarter after" or "five till" a certain hour. Brazilians sometimes use similar phrases and constructions. For times 15 minutes after the hour, you have the option of saying **e quinze** (ee *keen*-zee; and 15) or **e um quarto** (ee oong *kwah*-too; and a quarter) when you give the minutes. For times ending in 45, you can say either **quinze para** (*keen*-zee *pah*-dah; 15 to) before you give the hour or **e quarenta e cinco** (*ee* kwah-*den*-tah ee *sing*-koh; and 45) after you give the hour.

Midnight is **meia-noite** (*may*-ah *noh*-ee-chee), and *noon* is **meio-dia** (*may*-oh *jee*-ah; midday). In these cases — and when you say "it's one o'clock" — use **É** instead of **São,** because the number one and the words *midnight* and *noon* are singular:

✔ **É meia-noite.** (eh *may*-ah *noh*-ee-chee; It's midnight.)

✔ **É meio-dia.** (eh *may*-oh *jee*-ah; It's noon.)

✔ **É uma.** (eh *ooh*-mah; It's one.)

✔ **É uma e vinte.** (eh *ooh*-mah ee *veen*-chee; It's 1:20.)

Brazilians often use military time, especially in formal situations, like checking transportation schedules.

Here are some other words and phrases that indicate time:

- ✔ **hoje à noite** (*oh*-zhee ah *noh*-ee-chee; tonight)
- ✔ **noite** (*noh*-ee-chee; night)
- ✔ **cedo** (*seh*-doo; early)
- ✔ **tarde** (*tah*-jee; late)

If you're meeting up with someone, you may want to ask **A que horas?** (ah kee *oh*-dahz; At what time?) you'll be meeting. If you're responding to the question, you can leave out the **são** and just give the time: **Às nove e meia** (*noh*-vee ee *may*-ah; at 9:30).

When you've got talking about time down, here are some helpful phrases about timeliness;

- ✔ **O ônibus está atrasado?** (eh-*stah* ah-tdah-*zah*-doo ooh *oh*-nee-boos; Is the bus late?)
- ✔ **É sempre melhor chegar cedo.** (eh *sem*-pdee mel-*yoh* sheh-*gah seh*-doo; It's always better to arrive early.)
- ✔ **Acha que vamos poder chegar a tempo?** (*ah*-shah kee *vah*-mooz poh-*deh* sheh-*gah* ah *tem*-poh; Do you think we'll be able to arrive on time?)
- ✔ **O metrô de São Paulo é muito pontual.** (ooh meh-*tdoh* jee sah-ooh *pah*-ooh-loh eh moh-*ee*-toh pon-too-*ah*-ooh; The São Paulo subway system is very punctual.)
- ✔ **O atraso vai ser de uma hora.** (ooh ah-*tdah*-zoo *vah*-ee *seh* jee ooh-mah *oh*-dah; The delay will be an hour.)
- ✔ **Quase não chegamos a tempo.** (*kwah*-zee nah-ooh sheh-*gah*-mohz ah *tem*-poh; We almost didn't arrive in time.)

Monday, Tuesday: Weekdays

Dias da semana (*jee*-ahz dah seh-*mah*-nah; days of the week) in Portuguese seem bizarre at first.

According to legend, the Portuguese were obsessed with **feiras** (*fay*-dahz; outdoor food markets), and they sold different goods on each day of the **semana. Feiras** were so important to the Portuguese that they talked about the weekdays in reference to which **feira** was happening that day. Here are the days of the week:

- ✔ **domingo** (doh-*ming*-goo; Sunday)
- ✔ **segunda-feira** (seh-*goon*-dah-*fay*-dah; Monday)
- ✔ **terça-feira** (*teh*-sah-*fay*-dah; Tuesday)
- ✔ **quarta-feira** (*kwah*-tah-*fay*-dah; Wednesday)
- ✔ **quinta-feira** (*keen*-tah-*fay*-dah; Thursday)
- ✔ **sexta-feira** (*seh*-stah-*fay*-dah; Friday)
- ✔ **sábado** (*sah*-bah-doh; Saturday)

Brazilians also sometimes refer to the weekdays by their name without the word **feira. Segunda** is technically **segunda-feira** (*Literally:* second market — Monday is the second day of the week and a *market* or business day). But people often just say **segunda** or **quarta** or **sexta** — instead of **segunda-feira, quarta-feira,** and **sexta-feira.**

To say *on* a certain day of week, like *on Sunday,* say **no** (noh) or **na** (nah) before the day of the week — **no** if the day is a masculine word, **na** if it's feminine:

- ✔ **no domingo** (noh doh-*meeng*-goh; on Sunday)
- ✔ **na segunda** (nah seh-*goon*-dah; on Monday)
- ✔ **na terça** (nah *teh*-sah; on Tuesday)
- ✔ **na quarta** (nah *kwah*-tah; on Wednesday)
- ✔ **na quinta** (nah *keen*-tah; on Thursday)
- ✔ **na sexta** (nah *seh*-stah; on Friday)
- ✔ **no sábado** (noh *sah*-bah-doh; on Saturday)

Here are some examples:

- ✔ **Tem um show na quarta.** (tang oong *shoh* nah *kwah*-tah; There's a show on Wednesday.)

✔ **Na segunda, eu preciso trabalhar.** (nah seh-*goon*-dah eh-ooh pdeh-*see*-zoo tdah-bal-*yah;* On Monday, I need to work.)

✔ **Vamos sair na sexta?** (vah-mooz sah-*eeh* nah *seh*-stah; Should we go out on Friday?)

The following phrases are related to days:

✔ **hoje** (*oh*-zhee; today)

✔ **amanhã** (ah-mahn-*yah;* tomorrow)

✔ **na semana que vem** (nah seh-*mah*-nah kee *vang;* next week)

✔ **no fim de semana** (noh *feeng* jee seh-*mah*-nah; on the weekend)

✔ **no mês que vem** (noh *mehz* kee *vang;* next month)

Tracking the Calendar: Months and Dates

Whether you're planning dinner next week or a big appointment for work, you need to know how to talk your way around a calendar.

Naming the months

Note that, in Portuguese, the first letter of the name of each month isn't capitalized like it is in English:

✔ **janeiro** (zhah-*nay*-doh; January)

✔ **fevereiro** (feh-veh-*day*-doh; February)

✔ **março** (*mah*-soo; March)

✔ **abril** (ah-*bdee*-ooh; April)

✔ **maio** (*my*-oh; May)

✔ **junho** (*zhoon*-yoh; June)

✔ **julho** (*zhool*-yoh; July)

- **agosto** (ah-*goh*-stoh; August)
- **setembro** (seh-*tehm*-bdoh; September)
- **outubro** (oh-*too*-bdoh; October)
- **novembro** (noh-*vem*-bdoh; November)
- **dezembro** (deh-*zem*-bdoh; December)

To say *in* a certain month, use **em** (ang) plus the name of the month. Here are some example sentences:

- **Vou para o Brasil em maio.** (*voh pah*-dah ooh bdah-*zee*-ooh ang *my*-oh; I'm going to Brazil in May.)
- **Ela retornou do Canadá em novembro.** (*eh*-lah heh-toh-*noh* doo kah-nah-*dah* ang noh-*vehm*-bdoh; She returned from Canada in November.)

Picking a date

You may want to talk about days of the month and time of day for your odyssey.

To say *on* a certain day, use **no** (noh) plus the date. Use **no dia . . .** (date) **de . . .** (month) (noo *jee*-ah . . . jee . . .) to say *on such-and-such day of such-and-such month*. For example, **no dia quinze de setembro** (noo *jee*-ah *keen*-zee jee seh-*tehm*-bdoh) is September 15.

Check out some phrases that give you dates and times:

- **no dia três de outubro, às oito e vinte e cinco da manhã** (noo *jee*-ah *tdehz* jee oh-*too*-bdoh ahz *oh*-ee-toh ee *veen*-chee ee *sing*-koh dah mahn-*yah;* on October 3, at 8:25 a.m.)
- **no dia vinte e dois de agosto, às vinte horas** (noo *jee*-ah *veen*-chee ee *doh*-eez jee ah-*goh*-stoh ahz *veen*-chee *oh*-dahz; on August 22, at 8 o'clock p.m. [2000 hours])

✔ **no dia dezessete de dezembro, às vinte e uma horas e cinquenta minutos** (noo *jee*-ah dehz-eh-*seh*-chee jee deh-*zem*-bdoh ahz *veen*-chee ee *ooh*-mah *oh*-dahz ee sing-*kwen*-tah mee-*noo*-tohz; on December 17, at 9:50 p.m. [2150 hours])

✔ **no dia quatorze de maio, às dez e quinze da manhã** (noo *jee*-ah kah-*toh*-zee jee *my*-oh ahz *dez* ee *keen*-zee dah mahn-*yah;* on May 14, at 10:15 a.m.)

If you're referring to something in the past or far out in the future, your date requires an **ano** (*ah*-noh; year). Most years people refer to start with either 19 or 20. If the year is in the 1900s, say **mil novecentos e . . .** (*mee*-ooh noh-vee *sehn*-tohz ee; Nineteen . . .) If the year is in the current **século** (*seh*-koo-loh; century), say **dois mil e . . .** (*doh*-eez *mee*-ooh ee; Two-thousand . . .). Here are some examples of different years:

✔ **mil novecentos e cinquenta e dois** (*mee*-ooh noh-vee-*sehn*-tohz ee sing-*kwehn*-tah ee *doh*-eez; 1952)

✔ **mil novecentos e oitenta e três** (*mee*-ooh noh-vee-*sehn*-tohz ee oh-ee-*tehn*-tah ee *tdehz;* 1983)

✔ **mil novecentos e setenta e quatro** (*mee*-ooh noh-vee-*sehn*-tohz ee seh-*tehn*-tah ee *kwah*-tdoh; 1974)

✔ **dois mil e um** (*doh*-eez *mee*-ooh ee *oong;* 2001)

✔ **dois mil e seis** (*doh*-eez *mee*-ooh ee *say*-eez; 2006)

Money, Money, Money

O dinheiro (o jing-*yay*-doh; money) is the universal language. Or is that **o amor** (o ah-*moh;* love)?

Currency and prices

The **moeda** (moh-*eh*-dah; currency) in Brazil is called
o real (oh heh-*ah*-ooh), and the plural is **reais** (heh-
eyez). The **taxa de câmbio** (*tah*-shah jee *kahm*-bee-oh;
exchange rate) is about **um real** (oong heh-*ah*-ooh;
one real) to $0.45 (2.22 reais per US$1), and things are
generally more than **duas vezes** (*doo*-ahz *veh*-zeez;
two times) **mais barato** (*mah*-eez bah-*dah*-toh;
cheaper) than they are in the United States. Rejoice!

Brazilian slang for **dinheiro** is **grana** (*gdah*-
nah). **Estou sem grana** (eh-*stoh* sang *gdah*-
nah) means "I don't have any dough"
(*Literally:* I'm without dough).

Brazilian **reais** come in several bills, each with its own
color and an animal found in Brazil on the back. The
bills are as follows: R$1 (green/hummingbird), R$2
(blue/tortoise), R$5 (purple and blue/heron), R$10
(red/parrot), R$20 (yellow/golden-faced lion monkey),
R$50 (brown/jaguar), and R$100 (blue/grouper fish).

Coins come in R$1, R$0.50, R$0.25, R$0.10, R$0.05 and
R$0.01. The **um centavo** (*oong* sen-*tah*-voh; one-cent)
coin is tiny and is hardly worth anything. Stores more
often than not let you get away with paying to within
R$0.05 of the price, to avoid having the one-cent
pieces around. ***Remember:*** They're worth $\frac{1}{100}$ of one
real, or about $\frac{1}{5}$ of a U.S. penny.

To say a **preço** (*pdeh*-soo; the price), use the following formula: the number of **reais,** plus **e** (ee; and),
plus the number of **centavos** (sehn-*tah*-vohz; cents):

✔ **R$12,30: doze reais e trinta centavos** (doh-zee
    heh-*eyez* ee *tdeen*-tah sehn-*tah*-vohz; 12 reais
    and 30 cents)

✔ **R$4,60: quatro reais e sessenta centavos**
    (*kwah*-tdoh heh-*eyez* ee seh-*sehn*-tah sehn-*tah*-
    vohz; 4 reais and 60 cents)

✔ **R$2,85: dois reais e oitenta e cinco centavos**
    (*doh*-eez heh-*eyez* ee oh-ee-*tehn*-tah ee *sing*-koh
    sehn-*tah*-vohz; 2 reais and 85 cents)

Did you notice that instead of decimal points, Brazilians use commas? The decimal point is reserved in Portuguese for numbers beginning with a thousand — which looks like 1.000. So R$2.440 would be *two thousand, four hundred and forty reais.*

Getting money from banks and ATMs

When you need to get or exchange money, the following words are very important:

- ✔ **agência de viagens** (ah-*zhang*-see-ah jee vee-*ah*-zhangz; travel agency)

- ✔ **banco** (*bahn*-koh; bank)

- ✔ **caixa automático** (*kah*-ee-shah ah-ooh-toh-*mah*-chee-koh; ATM)

- ✔ **cartão de banco** (kah-*tah*-ooh jee *bahn*-koh; ATM card)

- ✔ **cartão de crédito** (kah-*tah*-ooh jee *kdeh*-jee-toh; credit card)

- ✔ **cartões internacionais** (kah-*toh*-eez *een*-teh-nah-see-ooh-*nah*-eez; international cards)

- ✔ **cheques de viagem** (*sheh*-keez jee vee-*ah*-zhang; traveler's checks)

- ✔ **taxa de câmbio** (*tah*-shah jee *kahm*-bee-oh; exchange rate)

- ✔ **retirar** (heh-chee-*dah*; to withdraw)

- ✔ **trocar** (tdoh-*kah;* to change money)

To ask where the nearest **banco** or **caixa automático** is, say:

- ✔ **Por favor, sabe onde tem um caixa automático?** (poh fah-*voh, sah*-bee ohn-jee *tang* oohng *kah*-ee-shah ah-ooh-toh-*mah*-chee-koh; Excuse me, do you know where there's an ATM?)

- ✔ **Por favor, tem um banco perto daqui?** (poh fah-*voh, tang* oong *bahn*-koh *peh*-toh dah-*kee;* Excuse me, is there a bank near here?)

Following up by asking whether the area the bank or ATM is located is reasonably **seguro** (seh-*goo*-doh; safe) is a good idea. Say **O local é seguro?** (ooh loh-*kah*-ooh eh seh-*goo*-doh; Is the area safe?). If you avoid withdrawing money at night, you should be fine.

Ask these questions when you want to change money:

- ✔ **Trocam dólares por reais?** (*tdoh*-kah-ooh *doh*-lah-deez poh hay-*eyez;* Do you change dollars for reais?)

- ✔ **A quanto está o dólar?** (ah *kwahn*-toh eh-*stah* ooh *doh*-lah; What's the rate for the dollar?)

- ✔ **Cobram taxa de comissão?** (*koh*-bdah-ooh *tah*-shah jee koh-mee-*sah*-ooh; Do you charge a commission fee?)

Brazilian vendors always seem to be out of **trocado** (tdoh-*kah*-doh; change). Getting large bills changed at the **banco,** right after you get it out of the **caixa automático,** is best. Vendors often ask **Tem trocado?** (*tang* tdoh-*kah*-doh; Do you have change?) when you pay, meaning "Do you have exact change? That would help me out."

Here's a sample conversation about changing money:

Silvio: **Por favor, trocam dólares por reais aqui?** (poh fah-*voh*, tdoh-kah-ooh *doh*-lah-deez poh heh-*eyez* ah-*kee?* Excuse me please, do you change dollars for reais here?)

Worker: **Trocamos.** (tdoh-*kah*-mooz; Yes, we do. [*Literally:* We change.])

Silvio: **Cobram taxa de comissão?** (*koh*-bdah-ooh *tah*-shah deh *koh*-mee-*sah*-ooh? Do you charge a fee?)

Worker: **Sim, é de dois por cento. Quanto quer trocar?** (*sing,* eh jee *doh*-eez poh-*sehn*-toh. *kwahn*-toh *keh* tdoh-*kah?* Yes, it's 2 percent. How much do you want to change?)

Silvio: **Cem dólares. A quanto está o dólar?**
(*sang doh*-lah-deez. ah *kwahn*-toh eh-*stah* ooh
doh-lah? $100. What's the rate for the dollar?)

Worker: **Está a dois reais e trinta e quatro.** (eh-
stah ah *doh*-eez heh-*eyes* ee tdeen-tah ee *kwah*-
tdoh. It's at 2.34 reais.)

Silvio: **Tá bom. Me dá em notas de dez?** (tah
boh-oong. mee *dah* ang *noh*-tahz jee *dehz?* That's
fine. Can you give it to me in bills of 10?)

Worker: **Tudo bem. Não tem problema.** (too-doh
bang. nah-ooh *tang* pdoh-*bleh*-mah. Okay. No
problem.)

Words to Know

Me dá . . . ?	mee <u>dah</u>	Can you give me . . . ?
notas	<u>noh</u>-tahz	bills
Não tem problema.	<u>nah</u>-ooh <u>tang</u> pdoh-<u>bleh</u>-mah	No problem.

Measuring Distances and Other Stuff

Measuring things like volume and weight is just as
universal. But if you happen to be an American, you'll
find that the way Brazilians measure stuff is different:
They use the metric system.

Check out Table 3-1 for the names of metric measure-
ments and some U.S. equivalents.

Table 3-1		Brazilian Measurements		
Type of Measure-ment	**Term**	**Pronunciation**	**Translation**	**U.S. Equiva-lent**
Distance	quilô-metro	kee-*loh*-meh-tdoh	kilometer	0.62 miles
Length	centí-metro	sehn-*chee*-meh-tdoh	centimeter	0.4 inches
Volume	litro	*lee*-tdoh	liter	1.06 quarts
Weight/mass	quilo	*kee*-loh	kilogram	2.2 pounds
Temper-ature	centí-grados	sehn-*chee*-gdah-dohz	degrees Celsius	⅖ × Celsius tempera-ture + 32

Chapter 4

Making New Friends and Enjoying Small Talk

*S*aying "hello" and "goodbye" is the nuts and bolts of any **língua** (*ling*-gwah; language). The **próximo passo** (*pdoh*-see-moh *pah*-soh; next step) is introducing yourself to people and introducing the people you're with. You'll want to tell people your **nome** (*noh*-mee; name), maybe even your **apelido** (*ah*-peh-*lee*-doh; nickname). Then comes the small talk about the weather, friends, work, or family.

When you're just learning a language, talking to people — even about the most basic things — can be a little stressful. But if you think about it, the first few minutes of talking to anybody new usually involves the same old questions. This chapter covers the questions that people who speak Portuguese are most likely to ask you, as well as the questions you'll probably want to ask them!

If you get a little lost in a conversation, these phrases will help you out:

- ✔ **Não entendi.** (*nah*-ooh ehn-ten-*jee;* I didn't understand.)
- ✔ **Oi?** (*oh*-ee; What did you say? [informal])
- ✔ **Poderia repetir, por favor?** (poh-deh-*dee*-ah heh-peh-*chee* poh fah-*voh;* Could you repeat that, please?)

A Few Ways to Say Hello and Goodbye

Saying "hello" is the bare necessity whether you're at home or in Brazil. Here are the most common ways of saying "hello" in Brazil:

- ✔ **Oi.** (*oh*-ee; Hi.)
- ✔ **Olá.** (oh-*lah;* Hello.)

If you're walking into a shop, restaurant, or hotel, it's more common to use "Good morning" or "Good afternoon" — just like in English:

- ✔ **Bom dia.** (*boh*-oong *jee*-ah; Good morning.)
- ✔ **Boa tarde.** (*boh*-ah *tah*-jee; Good afternoon/Good evening.)
- ✔ **Boa noite.** (*boh*-ah *noh*-ee-chee; Good evening/ Good night.)

In Brazil, **a tarde** (ah *tah*-jee; the afternoon) starts and ends a little bit later than you may be used to. The afternoon **começa** (koh-*meh*-sah; starts) around 2 p.m. and ends at about 8 p.m. Noon to 2 p.m. is **meio-dia** (may-oh-*jee*-ah; midday). But **ninguém** (ning-*gang;* no one) ever says **Bom meio-dia!** Go figure. They usually just say **Boa tarde.**

Another way of saying *hello* in Brazil is by asking directly, "How are you?" There are two ways of saying it:

- ✔ **Tudo bem?** (*too*-doh *bang;* How are you? *Literally:* Everything well?)

- ✔ **Tudo bom?** (*too*-doh *boh*-oong; How are you? *Literally:* Everything good?)

Here's how you answer:

- ✔ **Tudo bem.** (*too*-doh *bang;* I'm good. *Literally:* Everything well.)

- ✔ **Tudo bom.** (*too*-doh *boh*-oong; I'm good. *Literally:* Everything good.)

So what's the difference between **Tudo bem** and **Tudo bom,** you ask? Here's the big answer: There is none! They mean the same thing. But here's a great trick: If someone asks you **Tudo bem?** say **Tudo bom.** If it's **Tudo bom?** answer back **Tudo bem.** Just use the expression opposite the one that the other person used. People commonly combine some of these phrases, like **Olá, tudo bom?** (oh-*lah*, too-doh *bong;* Hello, how are you?) or **Oi, tudo bem?** (*oh*-ee, too-doh bong; Hi, how are you?).

The quick way to say goobye is simply to say **Tchau!** (chow; Ciao!). **Todo mundo** (*toh*-doo *moon*-doh; everyone. *Literally:* all world) in Brazil uses **Tchau,** in almost all situations. It's not like in English, where *Ciao!* can sound a little snobby sometimes. In Brazil, **Tchau** is used by everyone from the guy selling **aba-caxi** (ah-bah-kah-*shee;* pineapple) on the street to the **dono** (*doh*-noo; owner) of the restaurant where you're eating.

It's also very common in Brazil to say **Até** (ah-*teh;* until) plus another word when you think you'll see the person **de novo** (jee *noh*-voh; again). If you only **memorizar** (meh-moh-dee-*zah;* memorize) one of the following phrases, pick **Até logo.** It never fails.

✔ **Até logo.** (ah-teh *loh*-goo; See you later.)

✔ **Até mais.** (ah-teh *mah*-eez; See you.)

✔ **Até amanhã.** (ah-*teh* ah-mahn-*yah;* See you tomorrow.)

✔ **Até a semana que vem.** (ah-*teh* ah seh-*mah*-nah kee *vang;* See you next week.)

Some people like to say religious phrases, too:

✔ **Fique com Deus.** (*fee*-kee kohng *deh*-ooz; Take care. *Literally:* Be with God.)

✔ **Adeus.** (ah-*deh*-oohz; Goodbye. *Literally:* To God.)

A gente se vê (ah *zhang*-chee see *veh;* See you around) is a common slang-sounding of way of saying "bye" in a casual situation.

Introducing Yourself

Introducing yourself is easy as **torta de morango** (*toh*-tah jee moh-*dahng*-goh; strawberry pie). Here are a couple different ways to do it:

✔ **O meu nome é . . .** (ooh *meh*-ooh *noh*-mee eh; My name is . . .)

✔ **Eu sou o/a . . .** (*eh*-ooh *soh* ooh/ah; I'm . . .)

Use the *o* in front of your name if you're male and the *a* if you're female. Because *o* is the masculine way of saying "the" and *a* is the feminine "the," saying **Eu sou a Karen** is like saying, "I'm the Karen." It sounds **estranho** (eh-*stdahn*-yoh; weird) in English.

To ask someone his or her name, say **Qual é seu nome?** (*kwah*-ooh *eh* seh-ooh *noh*-mee; What's your name?). After someone asks you for your name, you can say **E o seu?** (ee ooh *seh*-ooh; And yours?).

If you want to **apresentar** (ah-pdeh-zen-*tah;* introduce) friends or family members after you introduce yourself, say:

Este é . . . (*es*-chee *eh;* This is . . . [name of man])

Esta é . . . (*eh*-stah *eh;* This is . . . [name of woman])

Estes são . . . (*es*-jeez *sah*-ooh; These are . . . [names of multiple people])

Estas são . . . (*eh*-stahz *sah*-ooh; These are . . . [names of women])

Here are some common introductions:

- ✔ **Este é o meu amigo.** (*es*-chee *eh* ooh *meh*-ooh ah-*mee*-goo; This is my friend. [male])

- ✔ **Esta é a minha amiga.** (*eh*-stah *eh* ah *ming*-yah ah-*mee*-gah; This is my friend. [female])

- ✔ **Estes são os meus amigos.** (*es*-cheez *sah*-ooh ooz *meh*-ooz ah-*mee*-gooz; These are my friends. [group of all men or men and women])

- ✔ **Estas são as minhas amigas.** (*eh*-stahz *sah*-ooh ahz *ming*-yahz ah-*mee*-gahz; These are my friends. [group of all women])

First Names, Last Names, and Nicknames

So when someone says **Qual é seu nome?** she's after your first name. If she says **Qual é seu nome completo?** (*kwah*-ooh *eh* seh-ooh *nah*-mee kohm-*pleh*-too; What's your full name? *Literally:* What's your complete name?), then she's after both your **primeiro nome** (pdee-*may*-doh *nah*-mee; name) and **sobrenome** (*soh*-bdee *nah*-mee; surname. *Literally:* over-names).

Brazilians always use **o** or **a** before a person's name: **A Mônica** (ah *moh*-nee-kah), **a Cláudia** (ah *klah*-ooh-jee-ah), **o Nicolas** (ooh nee-koh-*lahs*), **o Roberto** (ooh hoh-*beh*-too). It's like saying "the Steve" or "the Diane."

Os brasileiros (oohz bdah-zee-*lay*-dohz; Brazilians) are pretty **informal** (een-foh-*mah*-ooh; informal). They call their president just **Lula.** No one — not even on news shows — calls him **Senhor da Silva.** If people want to be formal, they'd say **o Presidente Lula** (ooh pdeh-zee-*dang*-chee *loo*-lah) — that's like saying "President George" for George Bush.

Brazilians prefer to stick to **primeiros nomes** (first names) in general, but when the situation is more formal, they use the terms **Senhor** (seen-*yoh;* Mr.) and **Senhora** (seen-*yoh*-dah; Mrs.) pretty much just like you use "Mr." and "Mrs." in English. When you're talking to your elderly **vizinho** (vee-*zeen*-yoh; neighbor), he's **Senhor** so-and-so. When a **casal** (kah-*zah*-ooh; couple) walks in to a real estate agency, they're called **Senhor e Senhora** (seen-*yoh* ee seen-*yoh*-dah; Mr. and Mrs.) so-and-so.

Brazilians always use **o/a** (the) before saying "Mr." or "Mrs." It's like saying "the Mr. Oliveira." Weird, right? Well, here goes:

- ✔ **o Senhor Oliveira** (ooh seen-*yoh* oh-lee-*vay*-dah; Mr. Oliveira)

- ✔ **o Senhor da Silva** (ooh seen-*yoh* dah *see*-ooh-vah; Mr. da Silva)

- ✔ **a Senhora Tavares** (ah seen-*yoh*-dah tah-*vah*-deez; Mrs. Tavares)

- ✔ **a Senhora Gimenes** (ah seen-*yoh*-dah zhee-*men*-ez; Mrs. Gimenes)

Another difference is that in Brazil, it's common to use **Senhor** and **Senhora** for young people — even teenagers. There's no term like *Miss* for younger women. And it's also normal for people to say **Senhor David** or **Senhora Luciana** — using the first name instead of the last name.

Imagine you're talking to the concierge of your hotel. He treats you with respect because it's his job to serve you. He asks you the following questions if you're a man:

✔ **O senhor mora aqui?** (ooh seen-*yoh moh*-dah ah-*kee;* Do you live here?)

✔ **O senhor está cansado?** (ooh seen-*yoh* eh-*stah* kahn-*sah*-doo; Are you tired?)

✔ **O senhor gosta do restaurante?** (ooh seen-*yoh goh*-stah doo heh-stah-oo-*dahn*-chee; Do you like the restaurant?)

And he asks you these questions if you're a woman:

✔ **A senhora gosta de dançar?** (ah seen-*yoh*-dah *goh*-stah jee dahn-*sah;* Do you like to dance?)

✔ **A senhora é americana?** (ah seen-*yoh*-dah eh ah-meh-dee-*kah*-nah; Are you American?)

✔ **A senhora vai para a praia?** (ah seen-*yoh*-dah vah-ee pah-dah ah *pdah*-ee-ah; Are you going to the beach?)

Now imagine that the speaker who asked you all these questions is just another fellow traveler — a Brazilian one. All the **o senhor's** and the **a senhora's** become **você** (voh-*seh;* you [informal]). **Você** is what you call people when you don't need to be formal.

Knowing Who, What, and Where

Key to any conversation are the basic question words **onde** (*ohn*-jee; where), **quando** (*kwahn*-doh; when), and **quanto** (*kwahn*-toh; how much). If you want to ask someone what something means, say **O que quer dizer . . . ?** (ooh *keh* keh jee-*zeh*). It literally means "What does . . . mean to say?"

Here are some other basic words to help you find information:

✔ **o quê?** (ooh *keh;* what?)

✔ **quem?** (kang; who?)

✔ **por quê?** (poh-*keh;* why?)

- ✔ **como?** (*koh*-moo; how?)
- ✔ **qual?** (*kwah*-ooh; which?)

The following are examples of how to use these words:

- ✔ **O que é isso?** (ooh *keh* eh *ee*-soh; What is that?)
- ✔ **Onde fica a praia?** (*ohn*-jee *fee*-kah ah *pdah*-ee-ah; Where is the beach?)
- ✔ **Quando é o concerto?** (*kwahn*-doh *eh* ooh kohn-*seh*-toh; When is the concert?)
- ✔ **Quem é ele?** (kang eh *eh*-lee; Who is he?)
- ✔ **Por que é assim?** (poh *keh* eh ah-*sing*; Why is it like that?)
- ✔ **Como ela é?** (*koh*-moo eh *eh*-lah; What is she like?)
- ✔ **Quanto é?** (*kwahn*-toh *eh*; How much does it cost?)
- ✔ **Qual carro é seu?** (*kwah*-ooh *kah*-hoh eh *seh*-ooh; Which car is yours?)

"Where Are You From?"

The first question you're likely to be asked in Brazil is **De onde você é?** (jee *ohng*-jee voh-seh *eh*; Where are you from?). Brazilians are very proud that people from all over the **mundo** (*moon*-doh; world) come to visit their country. They're always curious to imagine how **longe** (*lohn*-zhee; far) you came. They may also ask **De que país você é?** (jee kee pah-*eez* voh-seh *eh*; Which country are you from?).

Here's how you can answer:

- ✔ **Eu sou inglês** (*eh*-ooh *soh* eeng-*glehz*; I'm English.)
- ✔ **Eu sou da Inglaterra** (*eh*-ooh *soh* dah *eeng*-glah-*teh*-hah; I'm from England.)

Here are some countries and nationalities that you may find useful:

- ✔ **Estados Unidos** (ehs-*tah*-dooz ooh-*nee*-dooz; United States)
- ✔ **americano/a** (ah-meh-dee-*kahn*-oh/ah; American)
- ✔ **Canadá** (kah-nah-*dah;* Canada)
- ✔ **canadense** (kah-nah-*dehn*-see; Canadian)
- ✔ **Inglaterra** (eeng-glah-*teh*-hah; England)
- ✔ **inglês/inglesa** (eeng-*glehz/gleh*-sah; English)
- ✔ **Austrália** (ah-oo-*stdah*-lee-ah; Australia)
- ✔ **australiano/a** (ah-oo-stdah-lee-*ah*-noh/nah; Australian)
- ✔ **Alemanha** (ah-leh-*mahn*-yah; Germany)
- ✔ **alemão/ã** (ah-leh-*mah*-ooh/*mah;* German)
- ✔ **França** (*fdahn*-sah; France)
- ✔ **francês/francesa** (fdahn-*sehz*/fdahn-*seh*-zah; French)
- ✔ **China** (*shee*-nah; China)
- ✔ **chinês/chinesa** (shee-*nehz*/shee-*neh*-zah; Chinese)
- ✔ **Japão** (zhah-*pah*-ooh; Japan)
- ✔ **japonês/japonesa** (zhah-poh-*nez*/zhah-poh-*nes*-ah; Japanese)

Don't be surprised if a Brazilian from a touristy place like Rio responds **Eu já sabia** (*eh*-ooh jah sah-*bee*-ah; I knew it) when you say which country you're from. With so many tourists around, Brazilians get plenty of practice at pinpointing nationalities.

And a tip while I'm talking about Americans: A few Brazilians get offended by the term **americano.** They say, "We're Americans, too!" These folks prefer the term **norte-americano** (*noh*-chee-ah-meh-dee-*kah*-noh; North American).

Brazilians often tell you where they're from by using the nickname for people from their city or state. Here are the most common ones:

- ✔ **gaúcho/a** (gah-*ooh-sh*oh/ah; someone from Rio Grande do Sul state)

- ✔ **paulistano/a** (pow-lee-*stahn*-oh/ah; someone from the city of São Paulo)

- ✔ **paulista** (pow-*lee*-stah; someone from São Paulo state)

- ✔ **carioca** (kah-dee-*oh*-kah; someone from the city of Rio)

- ✔ **baiano/a** (bah-ee-*ah*-noh/ah; someone from Bahia state)

- ✔ **mineiro/a** (mee-*nay*-doh/ah; someone from Minas Gerais state)

Gente boa is a very common phrase in Brazil. It's used to describe people who are laid-back and down-to-earth. It literally means "good people," but you can use it to describe one person or a group of people. Here are a couple phrases you can use to win Brazilian friends:

- ✔ **Você é gente boa.** (voh-*seh* eh *zhang*-chee *boh*-ah; You're a really cool person.)

- ✔ **Os seus amigos são muito gente boa.** (oohz *say*-oohz ah-*mee*-gohz *sah*-ooh moo-*ee*-toh *zhang*-chee *boh*-ah; Your friends are really great.)

Here's a sample conversation:

Juliana: **Tudo bem? De onde você é?** (too-doh *bang*? jee *ohn*-jee voh-*seh* eh? How are you? Where are you from?)

Samir: **Sou americano.** (soh ah-meh-dee-*kahn*-oh; I'm American.)

Juliana: **De que lugar?** (jee kee loo-*gah*? From whereabouts?)

Samir: **De Ohio. E você, é daqui?** (jee oh-*hah*-ee-oh. ee voh-*seh, eh* dah-*kee*? From Ohio. And you, are you from here?)

Juliana: **Sim, sou gaúcha. De onde vem?** (sing, soh gah-*ooh*-shah. jee *ohn*-jee *vang*? Yes, I'm Gaúcha [from Rio Grande do Sul state]. Where are you coming from?)

Samir: **Do Rio. Vou passar uma semana aqui no Rio Grande do Sul.** (Doo *hee*-ooh. voh pah-*sah* ooh-mah seh-*mah*-nah ah-*kee* noh hee-ooh gdahn-jee doo *soo*. From Rio. I'm going to stay here in Rio Grande do Sul for a week.)

Juliana: **Ótimo. Está gostando do Brasil?** (*ah*-chee-moh. ehs-*tah* goh-*stahn*-doh doh bdah-*zee*-ooh? Great. Are you liking Brazil?)

Samir: **É claro! Estou adorando este pais.** (eh *klah*-doh! ehs-*toh* ah-doh-*dahn*-doh eh-schee pah-*eez*; Of course! I'm loving this country.)

Words to Know

De que lugar?	jee kee loo-<u>gah</u>	From where-abouts?
De onde vem?	jee ohn-jee <u>vang</u>	Which part of Brazil have you just been to?
Está gostando do Brasil?	eh-stah gohs-<u>tahn</u>-doh doh bdah-<u>zee</u>-ooh	Are you liking Brazil?
Estou adorando este pais.	ehs-toh ah-doh-dahn-doh eh-schee pah-eez	I'm loving this country.

Describing the World around You

Brazilians use **ser** (seh; to be) to describe the perma-
nent qualities of someone or something: "New York is
an island." "New York is big." "New York is pretty."
"She is married." "He is from New York." "He is rich
and nice." The verb **estar** (eh-*stah;* to be) is used in
situations where the quality being described is temporary, like being tired. Say you're talking about your
friend Ana, who has a rich husband. Don't worry
yourself over questions like "What if Ana's husband
goes bankrupt tomorrow?" or "What if Ana gets
divorced tomorrow?" Just remember the decade rule:
If the quality you're talking about seems like it will
last another ten years, use **ser.**

Describing permanent qualities: Ser

The verb **ser** (seh) is the one most often used in
Portuguese. It's an irregular verb (look at Chapter 2
for a quickie lesson on verbs). But it's the easiest
irregular verb there is in Portuguese. Check it out:

Conjugation	Pronunciation
Eu sou	*eh*-ooh *so*
Você é	voh-she *eh*
Ele/ela é	*eh*-lah/*eh*-lee *eh*
Nós somos	nohz *soh*-mooz
Eles/elas são	*eh*-leez/*eh*-lahz *sah*-ooh

I talked about what she looks like (physical character-
istics), what her profession is, and where she's from.

- **Ela é** (eh-lah *eh;* She is)
- **alta** (*ah*-ooh-tah; tall)
- **bonita** (boo-*nee*-tah; pretty)
- **loira** (*loy*-dah; blonde)

- ✔ **rica** (*hee*-kah; rich)

- ✔ **uma modelo** (*ooh*-mah moh-*deh*-loh; a model)

- ✔ **do Rio Grande do Sul** (doo *hee*-ooh *gdahn*-jee doo *soo;* from Rio Grande do Sul state)

Now that you know the verb **ser,** you can say a ton of things:

- ✔ **Eu sou homem.** (*eh*-ooh so oh-mang; I am a man.)

- ✔ **Eu sou da Califórnia.** (*eh*-ooh so dah kah-lee-*foh*-nee-ah; I am from California.)

- ✔ **Ele é muito alto.** (eh-lee *eh* moo-*ee*-toh *ah*-ooh-toh; He is very tall.)

- ✔ **Nós somos amigos.** (nohz *soh*-mooz ah-*mee*-gooz; We are friends.)

- ✔ **Elas são simpáticas.** (eh-lahz *sah*-ooh seem-*pah*-chee-kahz; Those women are nice.)

- ✔ **Ela é jovem.** (eh-lah *eh* zhoh-vang; She is young.)

- ✔ **Nós somos da Austrália.** (nohz *soh*-mooz dah ah-ooh-*stah*-lee-ah; We are from Australia.)

- ✔ **Eles são inteligentes.** (eh-leez *sah*-ooh een-teh-lee-*zhang*-cheez; They are smart.)

As you can see, **ser** goes perfectly with descriptions of things and people. Now glance at some basic description words you can use with **ser;** take a look at Table 4-1. These words are sure to come in handy.

Table 4-1	Adjectives Describing Permanent States	
Adjective	*Pronunciation*	*Translation*
alto	*ah*-ooh-toh	tall
baixo	*bah*-ee-shoh	short (height)
caro	*kah*-doh	expensive

(continued)

Table 4-1 *(continued)*

Adjective	Pronunciation	Translation
barato	bah-*dah*-toh	cheap
bom	*boh*-oong	good
mau	*mah*-ooh;	bad
curto	*kooh*-toh	short (length)
comprido	koom-*pdee*-doh	long
pequeno	peh-*keh*-noh	small
grande	*gdahn*-jee	big
fácil	*fah*-see-ooh	easy
difícil	jee-*fee*-see-ooh	difficult
divertido	jee-veh-*chee*-doo	fun
chato	*shah*-toh	boring/annoying
gordo	*goh*-doh	fat
magro	*mah*-gdoh	thin
jovem	*zhoh*-vang	young
velho	*vehl*-yoh	old

Take a look at this short exchange between friends:

Marco: **E como é Nova Iorque?** (ee *koh*-moh *eh* *noh*-vah *yoh*-kee? And what's New York like?)

Ana: **É muito grande. Também é muito bonita.** (eh moh-*ee* toh *gdahn*-jee. tahm-*bang* eh moh-*ee*-toh boo-*nee*-tah; It's really big. It's also really pretty.)

Marco: **É uma ilha, né?** (eh ooh-mah *eel*-yah, neh? It's an island, right?)

Ana: **Manhattan é uma ilha.** (Mahn-*hah*-tahn *eh* ooh-mah *eel*-yah; Manhattan is an island.)

Marco: **E foi para visitar a sua irmã, né?** (ee *foh*-ee pah-dah vee-see-*tah* ah soo-ah ee-*mah*, neh? And you went to visit your sister, right?)

Ana: **É. Ela é muito legal.** (*eh*. eh-lah *eh* moh-*ee*-toh leh-*gow*; Yeah. She's really cool.)

Marco: **Ela é casada?** (eh-lah *eh* kah-*zah*-dah? Is she married?)

Ana: **É. O marido dela é de Nova Iorque.** (*eh*. ooh mah-*dee*-doh *deh*-lah *eh* dah noh-vah *yoh*-kee. Yeah. Her husband is from New York.)

Marco: **Como ele é?** (*koh*-moh *eh*-lee *eh*? What is he like?)

Ana: **É rico e simpático!** (eh *hee*-koo ee seem-*pah*-chee-koh! He's rich and nice!)

Words to Know

Como é . . . ?	koh-moh eh	What is . . . like?
Nova Iorque	noh-vah yoh-kee	New York
muito	moh-ee-toh	really/very
grande	gdahn-jee	big
também	tahm-bang	too/also
ilha	eel-yah	island
foi	foh-ee	you went
para	pah-dah	in order to
visitar	vee-zee-tah	to visit

continued

Words to Know *(continued)*

irmã	ee-<u>mah</u>	sister
legal	leh-<u>gow</u>	cool
casada	kah-<u>zah</u>-dah	married
marido	mah-<u>dee</u>-doh	husband

If you want to sound a little more like a native speaker, use **né** at the end of a sentence to mean "Right?" (particularly in informal situations). **Né** is the contraction of **não é** (*nah-ooh eh; Literally:* is not), which can be used to mean the same thing as well. And use **É** at the beginning of a sentence to affirm a question someone just asked you. These words aren't necessary for you to learn, but they're fun, and Brazilians use them all the time!

Describing temporary qualities: Estar

The verb **estar** (eh-*stah*) is used most often to describe mood or physical state or physical location. Use **estar** to say you're **nervoso** (neh-*voh*-zoo; nervous) about something, that you're **doente** (doh-*en*-chee; sick), or that you're at the **banco** (*bahn*-koh; bank). Tomorrow, you may be "happy," "well," and "at work"!

To find out the different forms of **estar,** take a look:

Conjugation	Pronunciation
Eu estou	*eh*-ooh eh-*stoh*
Você está	voh-*seh* eh-*stah*
Ele/ela está	*eh*-lee/*eh*-lah eh-*stah*
Nós estamos	nohz eh-*stah*-mohz
Eles/elas estão	*eh*-leez/*eh*-lahz eh-*stah*-ooh

Here are some phrases using **estar:**

✔ **Ela está com fome.** (eh-lah eh-*stah* kong *foh*-mee; She is hungry.)

✔ **Você está gordinha.** (voh-*seh* eh-*stah* goh-*jing*-yah; You are a little chubby.)

✔ **Ela está com os sapatos vermelhos.** (*eh*-lah eh-*stah* kohng *ooz* sah-*pah*-tooz veh-*mel*-yooz; She is wearing red shoes.)

✔ **Nós estamos em Roma.** (nohz eh-*stah*-mohz ang *hoh*-mah; We are in Rome.)

✔ **Ela está de férias.** (*eh*-lah eh-*stah* jee *feh*-dee-ahz; She is on vacation.)

✔ **Nós estamos com fome.** (nohz eh-*stah*-mohz kohng *foh*-mee; We are hungry.)

✔ **Eu estou triste.** (*eh*-ooh eh-*stoh tdees*-chee; I am sad.)

✔ **Ela está no carro.** (*eh*-lah eh-*stah* noh *kah*-hoh; She is in the car.)

✔ **Eu estou em casa.** (*eh*-ooh eh-*stoh* ang *kah*-zah; I am at home.)

✔ **Eles estão no Brasil.** (*eh*-leez eh-*stah*-ooh noh bdah-*zee*-ooh; They are in Brazil.)

Speaking about Speaking

Now onto a really easy, fun verb: **falar** (fah-*lah;* to speak/to talk). Talking is, after all, how to really learn a language!

One of the most important phrases using falar is **Como se fala . . . ?** (*koh*-moo see *fah*-lah; How do you say . . . ?). This great phrase got me out of many linguistic jams.

You also use **falar** to refer to languages:

Eu falo inglês. (*eh*-ooh *fah*-loh eeng-*glehz;* I speak English.)

Take a look at Table 4-2 for a rundown of how to say the names of some of the world's major languages.

Table 4-2	Some of the World's Major Languages	
Language	*Pronunciation*	*Translation*
inglês	eeng-*glehz*	English
português	*poh*-too-*gez*	Portuguese
português de Portugal	poh-too-*gez* jee poh--too *gah*-ooh	Portuguese from Portugal
português do Brasil	poh-too-*gez* doh bdah-*zee*-ooh	Brazilian Portuguese
espanhol	eh-spahn-*yoh*-ooh	Spanish
russo	*hoo*-soh	Russian
chinês	shee-*nehz*	Chinese
francês	*fdahn-sehz*	French
italiano	ee-tah-lee-*ah*-noh	Italian
alemão	ah-leh-*mah*-ooh	German
árabe	*ah*-dah-bee	Arabic
hebreu	eh-*bdeh*-ooh	Hebrew

Some Brazilians prefer to say they speak **brasileiro** (bdah-zee-*lay*-doh; Brazilian) instead of **português** or **português do Brasil.**

Here are some easy ways to use **falar:**

> ✔ **Eu gostaria de falar chinês.** (*eh*-ooh goh-stah-*dee*-ah jee fah-*lah* shee-*nehz;* I would like to speak Chinese.)

✔ **Você fala muito rápido!** (voh-seh *fah*-lah moh-ee-toh *hah*-pee-doh; You talk really fast!)

✔ **Na reunião, nós falamos durante cinco horas!** (*nah* hay-*ooh*-nee-*ah*-ooh nohz fah-*lah*-mohz doo-*dahn*-chee *sing*-koh *oh*-dahz; During the meeting, we talked for five hours!)

✔ **Elas falam muito bem.** (eh-lahz *fah*-lah-ooh moh-*ee*-toh *bang;* They speak really well.)

✔ **É difícil falar o francês?** (eh jee-*fee*-see-ooh fah-*lah* ooh fdahn-sehz? Is it hard to speak French?)

✔ **Eu adoro falar o português.** (*eh*-ooh ah-*doh*-doo fah-*lah* ooh poh-too-*gez*. I love speaking Portuguese.)

✔ **Você fala quantas línguas?** (voh-seh *fah*-lah *kwahn*-tuz *ling*-gwahz; How many languages do you speak?)

The Good, the Bad, and the Humid: Weather

Though the **clima** (*klee*-mah; weather) in some parts of Brazil is nearly the same year-round, you'll find that Brazilians talk about the weather just as much as people from countries with more dramatic weather.

In southern Brazil, and as far north as São Paulo, the **inverno** (een-*veh*-noo; winter) can get very **frio** (*fdee*-ooh; chilly). It even **neva** (*neh*-vah; snows) some years in Rio Grande do Sul state, the southernmost part of the country. In northern and northeastern Brazil, the concept of having **quatro estações** (*kwah*-tdoh eh-stah-*soh*-eez; four seasons) seems very foreign to locals. For them, there are just two seasons: **temporada de chuva** (temp-oh-*dah*-dah jee *shoo*-vah; rainy season) and **temporada seca** (temp-oh-*dah*-dah *seh*-kah; dry season). At many schools across Brazil, instructors teach children only about **verão** (veh-*dah*-ooh; summer) and **inverno.**

Here are a few more seasonal terms:

- ✔ **outono** (oh ooh-*toh*-noo; autumn)
- ✔ **primavera** (pdee-mah-*veh*-dah; spring)
- ✔ **estação** (ehs-tah-*sah*-ooh; season)

Here's a conversation people might have about the weather in Brazil:

Vinicius: **Que calor! Estava esperando chuva.** (kee kah-*loh*! ehs-*dah*-vah ehs-peh-*dahn*-doh *shoo*-vah; It's so hot! I was expecting rain.)

Worker: **Não e só chuva aqui como todo mundo pensa.** (*nah*-ooh *eh* soh *shoo*-vah ah-*kee* koh-moh toh-doo moon-doh *pen*-sah; It's not all rain here like everyone thinks.)

Vinicius: **Porque estamos em temporada de chuva, né?** (poh-keh ehs-*tahm*-ohz ang tem-poh-*dah*-dah jee *shoo*-vah, neh? Because we're in the rainy season, right?)

Worker: **Estamos. Na verdade, não é típico ter sol em julho.** (ehs-*tah*-mohz. nah veh-*dah*-jee *nah*-ooh *eh chee*-pee-koh *teh* soh-ooh ang *joo*-lee-oh. We are. Actually, it's not normal to have sun in July.)

Vinicius: **Tenho sorte, então.** (tang-yoh *soh*-chee, en-*tah*-ooh; I'm lucky, then.)

Worker: **Sim, mas quem sabe — pela tarde pode precisar de um guarda-chuva.** (*sing*, *mah*-eez kang *sah*-bee — peh-lah *tah*-jee poh-jee pdeh-see-*zah* jee oong goo-*ah*-dah *shoo*-vah; Yeah, but who knows — in the afternoon you may need an umbrella.)

Vinicius: **Obrigado pela dica. Vou levar um.** (ohb-dee-*gah*-doh peh-lah *jee*-kah. *voh* leh-*vah* oong; Thanks for the tip. I'll bring one along.)

Words to Know

sol	<u>soh</u>-ooh	sun
quente	<u>kang</u>-chee	hot
calor	kah-<u>loh</u>	heat
frio	<u>fdee</u>-ooh	cold
chuva	<u>shoo</u>-vah	rain
chover	shoh-<u>veh</u>	to rain
guarda-chuva	goo-<u>ah</u>-dah <u>shoo</u>-vah	umbrella
nuvens	<u>noo</u>-vangz	clouds
úmido	<u>ooh</u>-mee-doh	humid
a umidade	ah ooh-mee-<u>dah</u>-jee	humidity

Figuring Out Family Connections

Brazilian families are very tight-knit; they tend to live in the same cities as their **pais** (*pah*-eez; parents) and **irmãos** (ee-*mah*-oohz; siblings/brothers and sisters) and to see each other at least once a week.

Take a look at Table 4-3 for more words to express family **relações** (heh-lah-*soh*-eez; relationships).

Table 4-3	Relatives	
Portuguese Word	*Pronunciation*	*English Word*
irmão	ee-*mah*-ooh	brother
irmã	ee-*mah*	sister

(continued)

Table 4-3 *(continued)*

Portuguese Word	Pronunciation	English Word
primo	*pdee*-moh	male cousin
prima	*pdee*-mah	female cousin
primos	*pdee*-mooz	cousins
avô	ah-*vah*	grandfather
avó	ah-*voh*	grandmother
avós	ah-*vohz*	grandparents
filho	*feel*-yoo	son
filha	*feel*-yah	daughter
filhos	*feel*-yooz	children
marido	mah-*dee*-doh	husband
mulher	mool-*yeh*	wife
neto	*neh*-toh	grandson
neta	*neh*-tah	granddaughter

In Brazil, street kids often call any adult **tia** (*chee*-ah; aunt) or **tio** (*chee*-ooh; uncle) — especially when they're asking for money or for help. If you find yourself in this situation, it's okay to give the child a small amount of money. Otherwise, just say, **Não posso** (*nah*-ooh *poh*-soo; I can't).

Giving Out Your Contact Information

After your first conversation with new friends, you may decide you'd like to keep in contact with them. Or they may ask you **Qual o seu número de telefone?**

(*kwah*-oo ooh seh-oo *noo*-meh-doh jee teh-leh-*fohn*-ee; What's your phone number?) You respond **O meu número de telefone é . . .** (ooh *meh*-oo *noo*-meh-doh jee teh-leh-*foh*-nee *eh;* My phone number is . . .).

Here are some other questions you can ask them. Notice the use of **seu** (your) and **meu** (my), which I talk about earlier in this chapter:

- ✔ **Qual é o seu sobrenome?** (*kwah*-ooh *eh* ooh *seh*-oo soh-bdee-*noh*-mee; What's your last name?)

- ✔ **Onde mora?** (ohn-jee *moh*-dah; Where do you live?)

- ✔ **Qual é o seu e-mail?** (*kwah*-ooh *eh* ooh *seh*-oo ee-*may*-oh; What's your e-mail?)

And here's how you can respond if you're asked these questions:

- ✔ **O meu sobrenome é . . .** (ooh *meh*-oo soh-bdee-*noh*-mee *eh;* My last name is . . .)

- ✔ **Eu moro . . .** (eh-ooh *moh*-doo; I live . . .)

- ✔ **O meu e-mail é . . .** (ooh *meh*-oo ee-*may*-oh *eh;* My e-mail is . . .)

Chapter 5

Enjoying a Drink and a Snack (or Meal!)

- -

In This Chapter

▶ Discussing food basics

▶ Enjoying the restaurant experience

- -

Está com fome? (eh-*stah koh*-oong *foh*-mee; Are you hungry?). **Quer comer?** (*keh* koh-*meh;* Do you want to eat?). This chapter helps you become acquainted with Brazilian cuisine and how to order it, talk about it, and enhance your enjoyment of it.

Bom Apetite! Enjoy Your Meal!

Mastering the dining basics is essential. But before you take a seat at the **mesa** (*meh*-zah; table), check out some of these place-setting terms:

- **garfo** (*gah*-foh; fork)
- **faca** (*fah*-kah; knife)
- **colher** (kool-*yeh;* spoon)
- **prato** (*pdah*-toh; plate)
- **prato fundo** (*pdah*-toh *foon*-doh; bowl)
- **copo** (*koh*-poo; cup/glass)
- **guardanapo** (gwah-dah-*nah*-poh; napkin)

Following are some basic items that you may want to
pedir (peh-*jee;* ask for) at a **restaurante** (heh-stah-
ooh-*dahn*-chee; restaurant) or someone's **casa** (*kah*-
zah; house):

- ✔ **sal** (*sah*-ooh; salt)

- ✔ **pimenta do reino** (pee-*mehn*-tah doo *hay*-noo;
  black pepper)

- ✔ **pimenta** (pee-*mehn*-tah; Brazilian hot sauce [hot
  red peppers soaking in oil]. *Literally:* pepper)

- ✔ **limão** (lee-*mah*-ooh; lime [Brazilians squeeze
  limão on everything!])

- ✔ **pão** (*pah*-ooh; bread)

- ✔ **gelo** (*zheh*-loh; ice)

Here are some useful phrases that you can use to talk
about food:

- ✔ **Eu adoro chocolate!** (*eh*-ooh ah-*doh*-doo shoh-
  koh-*lah*-chee; I love chocolate! *Literally:* I adore
  chocolate!)

- ✔ **Eu detesto ovos.** (*eh*-ooh deh-*teh*-stoh *oh*-vooz;
  I hate eggs. *Literally:* I detest eggs.)

- ✔ **Qual a sua comida favorita?** (*kwah*-ooh ah *soo*-
  ah koh-*mee*-dah fah-voh-*dee*-tah; What's your
  favorite food?)

- ✔ **Que tipo de comida gosta?** (kee *chee*-poh jee
  koh-*mee*-dah *goh*-stah; What type of food do you
  like?)

- ✔ **Qual prefere — a comida indiana ou a comida
  chinesa?** (*kwah*-ooh pdeh-*feh*-dee — ah koh-
  mee-dah een-*djee–ah-nah* oh-ooh ah koh-*mee*-
  dah shee-*neh*-sah; Which do you prefer — Indian
  or Chinese food?)

- ✔ **Você gosta de cozinhar?** (voh-*seh goh*-stah jee
  koh-zing-*yah;* Do you like to cook?)

- ✔ **Pode recomendar um bom restaurante por
  aqui?** (*poh*-jee heh-koh-mehn-*dah* oong *boh-oong*
  heh-stah-ooh-*dahn*-chee poh ah-*kee;* Can you
  recommend a good restaurant around here?)

Take a look at how to say the basic meals and parts of meals:

- **café da manhã** (kah-*feh* dah mahn-*yah;* breakfast. *Literally:* morning's coffee)

- **almoço** (*ah*-ooh-*moh*-soo; lunch)

- **jantar** (zhahn-*tah;* dinner)

- **entrada** (ehn-*tdah*-dah; appetizer. *Literally:* entry)

- **sobremesa** (soh-bdee-*meh*-zah; dessert)

And these are some phrases you can say at the table:

- **Que gostoso!** (kee gohs-*toh*-zoo; How amazingly delicious!)

- **É delicioso.** (eh deh-lee-see-*oh*-zoo; It's delicious.)

- **Está quente.** (eh-*stah kang*-chee; It's hot.)

- **Está frio.** (es-*stah fdee*-oh; It's cold.)

- **Bom apetite!** (boh-oong ah-peh-*tee*-chee; Bon appétit!)

- **Saúde!** (sah-*oo*-jee; Cheers! *Literally:* Health!)

Brazilians often just say **Quer?** (keh; Do you want?) to ask whether you want something. They may offer you a bite of their food by pointing to it and saying **Quer?**

At the Restaurant: Trying Local Foods

The classic Brazilian **comida** (koh-*mee*-dah; meal/food) is **simples** (*seem*-pleez; basic). It's a piece of **carne** (*kah*-nee; beef) served with **feijão** (fay-*zhow;* beans), **arroz** (ah-*hohz;* rice), and **salada** (sah-*lah*-dah; salad). In this section, I explore the restaurant experience and the food you can find there.

You can get a **refeição** (heh-fay-*sah*-ooh; meal) at five basic places in Brazil:

- ✔ **boteco** (boo-*teh*-koo; cheap restaurant where people also go to drink beer or take shots of liquor)
- ✔ **padaria** (pah-dah-*dee*-ah; bakery [at Brazilian **padarias,** you can also sit down for a meal])
- ✔ **lanchonete** (lahn-shoh-*neh*-chee; restaurant that specializes in hamburgers, sandwiches, and fruit juices)
- ✔ **restaurante por quilo** (heh-stah-ooh-*dahn*-chee poh *kee*-loh; self-serve buffet, pay per kilo [these are delicious, healthy, and cheap in Brazil])
- ✔ **restaurante** (heh-stah-ooh-*dahn*-chee; restaurant)

The first four options are for quick meals. They generally offer **sanduíches** (sahn-*dwee*-sheez; sandwiches), **hambúrgueres** (ahm-*booh*-geh- dez; hamburgers), **salgados** (sah-ooh-*gah*-dohz; savory pastries), and **pratos feitos** (pdah-tohz *fay*-tohz; a combo plate, usually rice, beans, meat, and salad).

If you need to go to the bathroom in a **restaurante,** you can just say **O banheiro?** (ooh bahn-*yay*-doh; The bathroom?). To be fancier, you can say **Por favor, onde fica o banheiro?** (poh fah-*voh* ohn-jee *fee*-kah ooh bahn-*yay*-doh; Where is the bathroom, please?)

Ordering at a restaurant

When you arrive at a **restaurante** (heh-stah-ooh-*dahn*-chee; restaurant), the **garçom** (gah-*sohng;* waiter) or **garçonete** (gah-soh-*neh*-chee; waitress) leads you to a **mesa** (*meh*-zah; table). He or she may ask you whether you want to **sentar** (sehn-*tah;* sit) **fora** (*foh*-dah; outside) or **dentro** (*dehn*-tdoh; inside).

Then the waiter or waitress gives you the **cardápio** (kah-*dah*-pee-oh; menu). You may see these sections:

✔ **entradas** (ehn-*tdah*-dahz; starters)

✔ **pratos principais** (*pdah*-tohz pdeen-see-*pah*-eez; main dishes)

✔ **bebidas** (beh-*bee*-dahz; drinks)

✔ **sobremesas** (soh-bdee-*meh*-zahz; desserts)

✔ **especialidades da casa** (eh-speh-see-ah-lee-*dah*-jeez dah *kah*-zah; house specialties)

When you're **pronto** (*pdohn*-toh; ready) to **pedir** (peh-*jeeh;* order. *Literally:* to ask for), you can just say either

✔ **Quero . . . por favor** (*keh*-doo . . . poh-fah-*voh;* I want . . . please)

✔ **Vou querer. . . .** (*voh* keh-*deh;* I will have. . . . *Literally:* I will want. . . .)

If you don't know what you want, you can ask the **garçom O que recomenda?** (ooh *keh* heh-koh-*mehn*-dah; What do you recommend?). If you want to go with what is recommended, say **OK, tá bom** (oh-*kay* tah *boh*-oong; Okay, I'll go with that. *Literally:* That's good.).

If you want to ask for something specific, say **Tem . . . ?** (tang; Do you have . . . ?). You can fill in the blank with one of the following words or phrases:

✔ **sopa** (*soh*-pah; soup)

✔ **salada** (sah-*lah*-dah; salad)

✔ **sanduíches** (sahn-doo-*ee*-sheez; sandwiches)

✔ **algo para crianças** (*ah*-ooh-goh *pah*-dah kdee-*ahn*-sahz; something for kids)

✔ **pratos vegetarianos** (*pdah*-tohz veh-zheh-teh-dee-*ah*-nohz; vegetarian dishes)

You can also use **Tem . . . ?** to ask whether a **prato** (*pdah*-toh; dish) contains a specific **ingrediente** (eeng-gdeh-jee-*ehn*-chee; ingredient) that you may or may not want:

✔ **Tem carne?** (tang *kah*-nee; Does it have meat in it?)

✔ **Tem frutos do mar?** (tang *fdoo*-tohz doo *mah;* Does it have any seafood in it?)

✔ **Tem azeite de dendê?** (tang ah-*zay*-chee jee dehn-*deh;* Does it have palm oil?)

If you know a **prato** has a specific **ingrediente** that you want **retirado** (heh-chee-*dah*-doh; taken out), say **sem . . .** (sang; without . . .). You can fill in the blank with one of the following words:

✔ **queijo** (*kay*-zhoh; cheese)

✔ **manteiga** (mahn-*tay*-gah; butter)

✔ **maionese** (mah-ee-oh-*neh*-zee; mayonnaise)

✔ **leite** (*lay*-chee; milk)

✔ **açúcar** (ah-*soo*-kah; sugar)

✔ **cebola** (seh-*boh*-lah; onion)

✔ **molho** (*mohl*-yoh; sauce)

✔ **óleo** (oh-*lay*-oh; vegetable oil)

✔ **alho** (*ahl*-yoh; garlic)

If you like your **carne** (*kah*-nee; meat) a certain way, you can ask for it to be

✔ **grelhada** (gdeh-ooh-*yah*-dah; grilled)

✔ **cozida** (koh-*zee*-dah; boiled)

✔ **frito** (*fdee*-toh; fried)

✔ **assado** (ah-*sah*-doh; sautéed)

Brazilian food is not **picante** (pee-*kahn*-chee; spicy). But you can ask for **pimenta** (pee-*mehn*-tah; hot chilies soaked in oil) or **molho de pimenta** (*mohl*-yoh jee pee-*mehn*-tah; hot sauce).

Ordering a drink

To help you wash down all the wonderful Brazilian food, you may want one of the following **bebidas** (beh-*bee*-dahz; drinks):

- ✓ **água sem gás** (*ah*-gwah *sang* gahz; still mineral water)

- ✓ **água com gás** (*ah*-gwah *koh*-oong *gahz;* sparkling mineral water)

- ✓ **Guaraná Antarctica** (gwah-dah-*nah* ahn-*tah*-chee-kah; Brazil's most popular brand-name soda, made from the Amazonian berry **guaraná — Antarctica** is the brand name)

- ✓ **Guaraná diet** (gwah-dah-*nah dah*-ee-chee; diet Guaraná)

- ✓ **Coca-Cola** (koh-kah *koh*-lah; Coke)

- ✓ **Coca light** (koh-kah *lah*-ee-chee; Diet Coke)

- ✓ **cerveja** (seh-*veh*-zhah; can of beer)

- ✓ **chope** (*shoh*-pee; light draft beer)

- ✓ **vinho** (*ving*-yoo; wine)

- ✓ **café** (kah-*feh;* coffee)

- ✓ **chá** (shah; tea)

- ✓ **leite** (*lay*-chee; milk)

If you go to a bar in Brazil, you may notice people saying **Mais um** (*mah*-eez *oong*) or **Mais uma** (*mah*-eez *ooh*-mah) a lot. The phrases mean "I'll have another" (*Literally:* More one).

The national drink of Brazil is the **caipirinha** (*kah*-ee-pee-*deen*-yah). It's made with **cachaça** (kah-*shah*-sah; sugarcane liquor), **gelo** (*zheh*-loh; ice), **limão** (lee-*mah*-ooh; lime) and **açúcar** (ah-*soo*-kah; sugar). You can also order a **caipifruta** (*kah*-ee-pee-*fdoo*-tah) — a caipirinha made from a fruit of your choice, instead of lime.

Brazilians love their juice and the average **restaurante** (heh-stah-ooh-*dahn*-chee; restaurant) has between 10 and 20 types of **sucos** (*soo*-kohz; fruit juices) to choose from. If you want to ask for the fruit in **suco** form, say **suco de . . .** (soo-koh *jee;* juice of . . .). Just plug one of these fruits into the blank:

- **laranja** (lah-*dahn*-zhah; orange)
- **abacaxi** (ah-bah-kah-*shee;* pineapple)
- **mamão** (mah-*mah*-ooh; papaya)
- **melancia** (meh-lahn-*see*-ah; watermelon)
- **goiaba** (goy-*ah*-bah; guava)
- **maracujá** (mah-dah-koo-*zhah;* passion fruit)
- **manga** (*mahn*-gah; mango)

My favorite **suco** is **cupuaçu** (koo-poo-ah-*soo;* milky white Amazonian fruit with a tangy taste).

Here are some helpful phrases that use the two drinking verbs **beber** and **tomar:**

- **É preciso beber muita água todos os dias.** (eh pdeh-*see*-zoh beh-*beh* moh-*ee*-tah *ah*-gwah toh-dooz ooz *jee*-ahz; It's necessary to drink a lot of water every day.)
- **Ele bebe muito.** (*eh*-lee *beh*-bee moh-*ee*-toh; He drinks a lot [of alcohol].)
- **O que quer para beber?** (ooh kee *keh* pah-dah beh-*beh;* What do you want to drink?)
- **Gostaria de tomar uma Coca-Cola?** (gohs-tah-*dee*-ah jee toh-*mah* ooh-mah koh-kah *koh*-lah; Would you like to have a Coke?)
- **Vamos tomar um drinque.** (*vah*-mohz toh-*mah* oong *dreeng*-kee; Let's have a drink/cocktail.)

First foods up: Salads and condiments

Saladas (sah-*lah*-dahz; salads) in Brazil are very basic if they come with your meal. But the salad bars, on the other hand, are stocked full of interesting items.

Brazilians tend not to mix salad ingredients like people do in the United States. Instead, they usually put the items side by side and then drizzle olive oil and red wine vinegar on top.

Here are some typical Brazilian items that you can expect to see at the salad bar:

- **alface** (ah-ooh-*fah*-see; lettuce)
- **rúcula** (*hoo*-koo-lah; arugula)
- **tomate** (toh-*mah*-chee; tomato)
- **tomate seco** (toh-*mah*-chee *seh*-koh; sun-dried tomato)
- **milho** (*meew*-yoh; corn)
- **palmito** (*pah*-ooh-*mee*-toh; heart of palm)
- **cenoura** (seh-*noh*-dah; carrots)
- **cebola** (seh-*boh*-lah; onion)
- **beterraba** (beh-teh-*hah*-bah; beets)
- **abobrinha** (ah-boh-*bdeeng*-yah; zucchini)
- **mozarela de búfala** (moh-tzah-*deh*-lah jee *boo*-fah-lah; fresh mozzarella)
- **queijo** (*kay*-zhoh; cheese)
- **azeite de oliva** (ah-*zay*-chee jee oh-*lee*-vah; olive oil)
- **vinagre** (vee-*nah*-gdee; red wine vinegar)
- **vinagrete** (vee-nah-*gdeh*-chee; chopped tomato, onion, and green bell pepper, with vinegar. *Literally:* vinaigrette [Brazilians put **vinagrete** on barbecued meat])

A note about **alface:** Brazilians call iceberg lettuce **alface americano** (ah-ooh-*fah*-see ah-meh-dee-*kah*-noh; American lettuce)! That's because iceberg lettuce is more popular in the United States than it is in Brazil.

On to the main course

The most famous Brazilian dish is called **feijoada** (fay-zhoh-*ah*-dah; bean/pig-parts stew). It has **orelha de porco** (oh-*dehl*-yah jee *poh*-koo; pig's ears) and even **joelho de porco** (zhoh-*ehl*-yoh jee *poh*-koo; pig's knees), in addition to the more **nobre** (*noh*-bdee; good quality. *Literally:* noble) parts of the pig.

Here's an index of classic Brazilian food items and dishes — besides **churrasco** (choo-*hah*-skoo; Brazilian barbeque), which I cover in the "Basking in Brazilian barbeque" section, and **feijoada:**

- ✔ **limão** (lee-*mah*-ooh; lime): Brazilians squeeze lime on just about anything, especially the classic meal combo of rice, beans, and skirt beef steak. It's also used in juices and desserts. Don't try to ask for a lemon in Brazil — they don't have any.

- ✔ **coco** (*koh*-koh; coconut): Brazilians love coconut. They drink coconut juice out of a whole green coconut, through a straw. Men chop off a top slice of the coconut with a machete and then sell it for 1 real (about 30¢) on the beach and on the street. **Coco** is also used in lots of main dishes from Bahia state.

- ✔ **pão de queijo** (*pah*-ooh jee *kay*-zhoh; cheese bread): Sold either as little balls or in pieces the size of a biscuit, it's unbelievably delicious.

- ✔ **moqueca** (moh-*keh*-kah; thick fish stew from Bahia state): This stew is made with **azeite de dendê** (ah-*zay*-chee jee dehn-*deh;* palm oil), which is hard on some stomachs, and **leite de coco** (*lay*-chee jee *koh*-koo; coconut milk).

- ✔ **acarajé** (ah-*kah*-dah-*zheh;* deep-fried black-eyed pea cakes, filled with tiny unpeeled shrimp, raw onions, tomato, green pepper, and peanut sauce): This popular dish from Bahia state is sold on beaches and on the street. It's also made with **azeite de dendê.**

✔ **coxinha** (koh-*sheeng*-yah; mashed potatoes, fried, shaped into a teardrop, with shredded chicken inside): You can find these at most corner **botecos** (boo-*teh*-kooz; cheap restaurants) or bakeries in Brazil.

✔ **açaí na tigela com granola** (ah-sah-*ee* nah tee-*zheh*-lah *koh*-oong gdah-*noh*-lah; Amazonian fruit sorbet in a large bowl, topped with granola and sometimes honey): This is the favored beach food of Brazilian surfers. **Açaí** is a small eggplant-colored berry.

✔ **farofa** (fah-*doh*-fah; toasted manioc flour mixed in with bits of fried pork and scrambled eggs): This is served with **feijoada** or on the side with your steak. Mmmm. A not-to-miss!

✔ **mandioca frita** (mahn-jee-*ah*-kah *fdee*-tah; fried yucca): This is my favorite Brazilian food item. It's way better than French fries!

✔ **X-salada** (*sheez* sah-*lah*-dah; cheeseburger with lettuce and tomato. *Literally:* cheese with salad): The letter *x* is pronounced *sheez* in Portuguese, which sounds like the English word *cheese,* so they just write the letter *x*. Brazilians always have a sense of humor.

Basking in Brazilian barbeque

You can't talk about Brazilian food without mentioning the beloved **churrascaria** (choo-*hah*-skeh-*dee*-ahz; Brazilian-style barbeque joint). It's a **comer à vontade** (koh-*meh* ah vohn-*tah*-jee; all-you-can-eat) affair.

Waiters come by your **mesa** (*meh*-zah; table) with about ten different **cortes** (*koh*-cheez; cuts) of meat every five minutes or so. Sometimes they give you a round card that's **verde** (*veh*-jee; green) on one side and **vermelho** (veh-*mehl*-yoh; red) on the other. When you want to **comer mais** (koh-*meh mah*-eez; eat more), place the card with the **verde** side up. And when you're **satisfeito** (sah-tees-*fay*-toh; full), be sure to have the **vermelho** side showing. Otherwise, it'll be hard to fend off the **garçons** (gah-*soh*-oongz; waiters)!

Here are the typical **cortes** the **garçons** may bring by your **mesa:**

- **picanha** (pee-*kahn*-yah; rumpsteak)
- **alcatra** (ow-*kah*-tdah; top sirloin)
- **fraldinha** (fdah-ooh-*jeen*-yah; flank steak)
- **lingüiça** (ling-*gwee*-sah; Brazilian chorizo-style sausage)
- **lombo** (*lohm*-boh; pork loin)
- **coxa de frango** (*koh*-shah jee f*dahn*-goh; chicken thighs)
- **peito de frango** (*pay*-toh jee f*dahn*-goh; chicken breast)
- **coração de frango** (koh-dah-*sah*-ooh jee f*dahn*-goh; chicken hearts)
- **cordeiro** (koh-*day*-doh; lamb)

Farinha (fah-*ding*-yah; manioc flour) is simply **esquisito** (ehs-kee-*zee*-toh; bizarre) the first time you encounter it. Flour you dip your meat into? I personally didn't like **farinha** for about a year. But now when I eat a steak in the United States, I miss it. It's an acquired taste. And when you've acquired the taste, it's impossible to **viver sem** (vee-*veh sang;* live without).

Vegetarianos (veh-zheh-teh-dee-*ah*-nohz; vegetarians), never fear: **Churrascarias** always have a wonderful salad buffet.

Doing dessert

End the meal with some **sobremesa** (soh-bdee-*meh*-zah; dessert). Here are some of my favorites:

- **bolo de laranja** (boh-loo jee lah-*dahn*-zhah; orange-flavored pound cake)
- **bolo de limão** (boh-loo jee lee-*mah*-ooh; lime-flavored pound cake)
- **flan** (fluhn; flan custard)

✔ **mousse de maracujá** (mooz jee mah-dah-koo-*jah;* passion-fruit mousse)

✔ **mousse de chocolate** (mooz jee sho-koh-*lah*-chee; chocolate mousse)

✔ **sorvete** (soh-*veh*-chee; ice cream)

✔ **iogurte** (ee-oh-*goo*-chee; yogurt)

✔ **Romeu e Julieta** (*hoh*-mee-ooh ee zhoo-lee-*eh*-tah; guava paste with a piece of hard cheese. *Literally:* Romeo and Juliet)

✔ **pizza doce** (*pee*-tzah *doh*-see; sweet pizza)

In Brazil it's common for pizza joints to offer several dessert pizzas. **Chocolate e morango** (sho-koh-*lah*-chee ee; chocolate and strawberry) is an experience not to be missed.

You may want a **cafezinho** (kah-feh-*zeen*-yoh; shot of Brazilian coffee, served in a tiny cup or glass and sweetened with a lot of sugar) to go with your **sobremesa.** In good restaurants, you can ask for your coffee to be **sem açúcar** (sang ah-*soo*-kah; unsweetened). And if you're really in a decadent mood, you can ask for **chantily** (shan-chee-*lee;* whipped cream) with your coffee.

Paying the bill

Paying the bill isn't the most fun part of eating out, but this dialogue can help you practice what to say when the time comes.

Alberto: (To the waiter) **A conta, por favor.** (ah *kohn*-tah, poh fah-*voh*. The check, please.)

Waiter: **Vou trazê-la agora.** (voh tdah-*zeh*-lah ah-*goh*-dah. I'll bring it now.)

Alberto: **Aceita cartão?** (ah-*say*-tah kah-*tah*-ooh? Do you accept credit cards?)

Waiter: **Aceitamos.** (ah-say-*tah*-mohz; Yes, we do. *Literally:* We accept.)

Alberto: (After he sees the bill) **Que caro. Noventa e sete reais?** (kee *kah*-doh. noh-*vehn*-tah ee *seh*-chee hay-*eyes?* How expensive. Ninety-seven reais [about $30]?)

Marina: **O serviço está incluído?** (ooh seh-*vee*-soh eh-*stah* eeng-kloo-*ee*-doo? Is the tip included?)

Alberto: **Ah — foi por isso. É taxa de quinze por cento.** (*ah* — *foh*-ee poh *ees*-soh. eh *tah*-shah jee *keen*-zee poh *sehn*-toh; Ah — that's why. It's 15 percent.)

Marina: (To the waiter, after the credit-card receipt comes back) **Tem caneta?** (*tang* kah-*neh*-tah? Do you have a pen?)

Brazilians generally don't leave a **gorjeta** (goh-*zheh*-tah; American-type tip) at restaurants. If service is exceptional, you can leave a **gorjeta** of 10 percent. Sometimes a 10 percent or 15 percent tip is required and included in the **conta** (*kohn*-tah; bill). You can tell because it says **serviço incluído** (seh-*vee*-soh een-kloo-*ee*-doh; tip included). *Sales tax* on a **conta** shows up as **I.V.A.** (*ee*-vah).

Words to Know

a conta	ah <u>kohn</u>-tah	the bill
vou	<u>voh</u>	I will
trazê-lo	tdah-<u>zeh</u>-loh	bring it
aceita	ah-<u>say</u>-tah	do you accept/ he or she accepts
cartão	kah-<u>tah</u>-ooh	credit card (Literally: card)
aceitamos	ah-say-<u>tah</u>-mohz	we accept

uma porção	<u>ooh</u>-mah poh-<u>sah</u>-ooh	an order (one portion of food)
cada	<u>kah</u>-dah	each
caro	<u>kah</u>-doh	expensive
o serviço	ooh seh-<u>vee</u>-soh	-obligatory tip (*Literally:* service)
incluído	eeng kloo-<u>ee</u>-doo	included
foi por isso	<u>foh</u>-ee poh <u>dee</u>-ssoh	that's why
caneta	kah-<u>neh</u>-tah	pen

Chapter 6

Shop 'Til You Drop

. . . .

In This Chapter

▶ Buying and wearing clothes

▶ Checking out Brazilian handicrafts

▶ Shopping for food

▶ Expressing opinions: Good, better, best

▶ Paying and bargaining

. . . .

*I*n Brazil or anywhere, you can shop for **prazer** (pdah-*zeh;* pleasure) or out of **necessidade** (neh-seh-see-*dah*-jee; necessity). This chapter takes you out shopping on the town, with all the vocab you need to know.

Finding Places to Shop

You can **fazer compras** (fah-*zeh kohm*-pdahz; shop) in these main ways:

▶ **uma loja na rua** (*ooh*-mah *loh*-zhah nah *hoo*-ah; a store on the street)

▶ **uma feira** (*ooh*-mah *fay*-dah; an outdoor market)

▶ **supermercados** (*soo*-peh-meh-*kah*-dooz; supermarkets)

▶ **um shopping** (*oong shoh*-ping; a shopping mall)

Brazil's **shoppings** (*shoh*-pings; shopping malls) are very similar to the malls you've been to wherever you're from. They have

- ✔ **lojas de roupas** (*loh*-zhahz jee *hoh*-pahz; clothing stores)

- ✔ **livrarias** (lee-vdah-*dee*-ahz; bookstores)

- ✔ **farmácias** (fah-*mah*-see-ahz; drugstores)

- ✔ **lojas de CDs** (*loh*-zhahz jee seh-*dehz*; CD stores)

- ✔ **salas de cinema** (*sah*-lahz jee see-*neh*-mah; movie theaters)

- ✔ **praças de alimentação** (*pdah*-sahz jee ah-lee-mehn-tah-*sah*-ooh; food courts)

In Brazil, **shoppings** are more associated with the middle and upper classes. Those people with less **dinheiro** (jeen-*yay*-doh; money) prefer **lojas na rua** or **feiras** — where **coisas** (*koy*-zahz; things) are **mais barato** (*mah*-eez bah-*dah*-toh; cheaper).

Out for the Perfect Outfit

When you enter a Brazilian **loja** (*loh*-zhah; store) looking for **roupas** (*hoh*-pahz; clothes), expect to hear **Posso ajudar?** (*poh*-soo ah-zhoo-*dah*; Can I help you?). After **Posso ajudar?** the **atendente** (ah-tehn-*dehn*-chee; salesperson) may say

- ✔ **Está procurando algo em específico?** (eh-*stah* pdoh-koo-*dahn*-doh *ah*-ooh-goh ang eh-speh-*see*-fee-koh; Are you looking for something in particular?)

- ✔ **Já conhece a nossa loja?** (zhah kohn-*yeh*-see ah *noh*-sah *loh*-zhah; Are you already familiar with our store?)

- ✔ **Temos uma promoção.** (*teh*-mohz *ooh*-mah pdoh-moh-*sah*-ooh; We're having a sale.)

And here are some things you can say to the **atendente**:

- ✔ **Estou só olhando.** (eh-*stoh* soh ohl-*yahn*-doh; I'm just looking.)

✔ **Estou procurando . . .** (eh-*stoh* pdoh-koo-*dahn*-doh; I'm looking for . . .)

✔ **Tem . . . ?** (tang; Do you have . . . ?)

Skirts and shirts: Which to choose

Now for the goods. **De que precisa?** (jee *keh* pdeh-*see*-zah; What do you need?). You can tell the salesperson **Estou procurando** (eh-*stoh* pdoh-koo-*dahn*-doh; I'm looking for) one of the following items:

✔ **calças** (*cow*-sahz; pants)

✔ **calça jeans** (*cow*-sah *jeenz;* jeans)

✔ **blusa** (*bloo*-zah; woman's shirt)

✔ **camisa** (kah-*mee*-zah; man's shirt)

✔ **camiseta** (kah-mee-*zeh*-tah; T-shirt)

✔ **saia** (*sah*-ee-ah; skirt)

✔ **vestido** (ves-*chee*-doo; dress)

✔ **cinto** (*seen*-too; belt)

✔ **meias** (*may*-ahz; socks)

✔ **sapatos** (sah-*pah*-tohz; shoes)

✔ **relógio** (heh-*law*-zhee-oh; watch)

✔ **chapéu** (shah-*peh*-ooh; hat)

You may want to specify a **tamanho** (tah-*mahn*-yoh; size). In Brazil, **os tamanhos** are either European (when they're in numbers — both clothing and shoes) or generic, from small to extra large:

✔ **pequeno (P)** (peh-*keh*-noh; small)

✔ **médio (M)** (*meh*-jee-oh; medium)

✔ **grande (G)** (*gdahn*-jee; large)

✔ **extra grande (GG)** (*ehz*-tdah *gdahn*-jee; extra large)

✔ **tamanho único** (tah-*mahn*-yoh *oo*-nee-koh; one size fits all)

Brazilian sizes are smaller than in North America and in some European countries. The same size shirt will be a medium, say, in the United States but a large in Brazil. I'm a semi-tall gal who tries to exercise regularly, and sadly, I most often had to buy the **grande** or **extra grande** sizes. So don't feel like you suddenly have to go on a **regime** (heh-*zhee*-mee; diet) after you hit the Brazilian stores!

You can also request a certain **cor** (koh; color):

- ✔ **branco** (*bdahn*-koh; white)
- ✔ **preto** (*pdeh*-toh; black)
- ✔ **vermelho** (veh-*meh*-ooh-yoh; red)
- ✔ **verde** (*veh*-jee; green)
- ✔ **amarelo** (ah-mah-*deh*-loo; yellow)
- ✔ **azul** (ah-*zoo*; blue)
- ✔ **marrom** (mah-*hoh*-oong; brown)
- ✔ **rosa** (*hoh*-zah; pink)
- ✔ **roxo** (*hoh*-shoo; purple)
- ✔ **laranja** (lah-*dahn*-zhah; orange)

If you want a different shade, just add **claro** (*klah*-doh; light) or **escuro** (eh-*skoo*-doh; dark) after the name of the color:

- ✔ **azul claro** (ah-*zoo klah*-doh; light blue)
- ✔ **vermelho escuro** (veh-*meh*-ooh-yoh eh-*skoo*-doh; dark red)

So what happens if your **cinto** or **camiseta** is too small? Or too big? You could say:

- ✔ **É pequeno demais.** (eh peh-*keh*-noh jee-*my*-eez; It's too small.)
- ✔ **É grande demais.** (eh *gdahn*-jee jee-*my*-eez; It's too big.)

Putting the word **demais** after a word is like adding the word *too* or *really* in front of an English word. Check it out:

- ✔ **É caro demais.** (eh *kah*-doh jee-*my*-eez; It's too expensive.)

- ✔ **É bonito demais.** (*eh* boo-*nee*-too jee-*my*-eez; It's really beautiful.)

É bom demais! (eh *boh-oong* jee-*my*-eez; It's fantastic!) is a common phrase that literally means "It's too good!"

Trying it on

The verb for trying on clothes is **experimentar** (eh-*speh*-dee-mehn-*tah*). It's easy to remember — what does the word look like? **Tá certo** (tah *seh*-toh; That's right) — *experiment*. In Portuguese, you "experiment" with new **cores** (*koh*-deez; colors) and new looks by **experimentando** (eh-speh-dee-mehn-*tahn*-doh; trying on) **artigos de roupa** (ah-*chee*-gohz jee *hoh*-pah; articles of clothing). Here are some common phrases using **experimentar**:

- ✔ **Quer experimentar . . . ?** (*keh* eh-*speh*-dee-mehn-*tah;* Would you like to try/try on . . . ?)

- ✔ **Gostaria de experimentá-lo?** (goh-stah-*dee*-ah jee eh-*speh*-dee-mehn-*tah*-loh; Would you like to try it on?)

- ✔ **Posso experimentar . . . ?** (*poh*-soo eh-*speh*-dee-mehn-*tah;* Can I try/try on . . . ?)

- ✔ **Posso experimentar essa blusa?** (*pah*-soo eh-*speh*-dee-mehn-*tah* eh-sah *bloo*-zah; Can I try on this [women's] shirt?)

- ✔ **Tem que experimentar . . .** (*tang* kee eh-*speh*-dee-mehn-*tah;* You've got to try/try on . . .)

- ✔ **É só experimentar.** (eh *soh* eh-*speh*-dee-mehn-*tah;* It won't hurt just to try it/try it on. *Literally:* It's just trying.)

After you leave the **provador** (pdoh-vah-doh; dressing room), the salesperson may ask you **Quer levar?** (keh leh-*vah;* Would you like to get it?). Here are some answers:

- **Vou levar.** (voh leh-*vah;* I'll take it.)

- **Não, não vou levar, mas obrigado/a.** (*nah*-ooh, *nah*-ooh voh leh-*vah,* mah-eez oh-bdee-*gah*-doh/ ah; No, I'm not going to get it, but thanks.)

Here's a conversation you might have with a salesperson:

Dudu: **Gosto muito desses**. (*goh*-stoo moh-*ee*-too *deh*-seez; I really like these.)

Salesperson: **São bonitos. Quer experimentar?** (*sah*-ooh boo-*nee*-tooz. *keh* eh-*speh*-dee-mehn-*tah;* They're nice. Do you want to try them on?)

Dudu: **Posso?** (*poh*-soo; Can I?)

Salesperson: **Claro.** (*klah*-doo; Of course.)

Dudu: **Obrigado. São muito legais.** (oh-bdee-*gah*-doh. *sah*-ooh moh-*ee*-toh lay-*gah*-eez. Thanks. They're really cool.)

Salesperson: **Estou vendendo muito desse modelo.** (eh-stoh vehn-*dehn*-doh moh-*ee*-too *deh*-see moh-*deh*-loo; I'm selling a lot of that type.)

Dudu: **Quanto custam?** (*kwahn*-toh *koo*-stah-ooh; How much do they cost?)

Salesperson: **São oito reais. Quer levar?** (*sah*-ooh oh-*ee*-toh heh-*eyes*. *keh* leh-*vah;* Eight reais. You wanna take them?)

Dudu: **Vou, sim. Tem troco para dez reais?** (voh *sing*. tang *tdoh*-koo pah-dah *dehz* heh-*eyes;* Yeah. Do you have change for ten reais?)

Words to Know

gosto	<u>goh</u>-stoo	I like
desses	<u>deh</u>-seez	of these
estou	eh-<u>stoh</u>	I am
vendendo	vehn-<u>dehn</u>-doh	selling
troco	<u>tdoh</u>-koo	change (for money)

The verb **gostar** (goh-*stah;* to like) is always followed by **de** (jee), which means "of." But in English, saying something like "I like of these" just sounds weird, so when you translate **Gostar desses** (I like these) to English, just leave out the *of.*

Exploring Brazilian Treasures

Brazilian **mercados** (meh-*kah*-dooz; markets) have plenty of **artesanato** (*ah*-teh-zah-*nah*-toh; handicrafts) that you may want as **lembranças** (lehm-*bdahn*-sahz; souvenirs), such as **redes** (*heh*-jeez; hammocks) and **berimbaus** (beh-deem-*bah*-ooz; musical instruments from the state of Bahia).

Also in Bahia are the famous colorful **fitas de Bonfim** (*fee*-tahz jee *boh*-oong-*feeng;* ribbons of Bonfim). These ribbons, which have religious sayings on them, come from a church called Bonfim in the city of Salvador. When you buy a **fita,** the seller ties it around your wrist and tells you to make a wish. The vendor then warns you **nunca** (*noon*-kah; never) to take it off; otherwise, you'll be cursed with **má sorte** (*mah soh*-chee; bad luck). On the upside, if you let it disintegrate naturally, they say the wish you made will come true!

Check out some other classic Brazilian souvenirs:

- **uma pintura** (*ooh*-mah peen-*too*-dah; a painting)
- **um biquíni** (oohng bee-*kee*-nee; a bikini)
- **bijuteria** (bee-*zhoo*-teh-*dee*-ah; jewelry)
- **anéis** (ah-*nay*-eez; rings)
- **brincos** (*bdeeng*-kohz; earrings)
- **colares** (koh-*lah*-deez; necklaces)
- **uma canga com a bandeira brasileira** (*ooh*-mah *kahn*-gah kohng ah bahn-*day*-dah bdah-zee-*lay*-dah; a beach sarong used as a towel or skirt, printed with the Brazilian flag)
- **música brasileira** (*moo*-zee-kah bdah-zee-*lay*-dah; Brazilian music)
- **produtos dos índios** (pdoh-*doo*-tohz dohz *een*-jee-ohz; products made by native Brazilian tribes)
- **pó de guaraná** (*poh* jee gwah-dah-*nah;* guarana berry powder used to make a traditional natural energy drink)
- **uma camiseta de um time de futebol** (*ooh*-mah kah-mee-*zeh*-tah jee oong *chee*-mee jee foo-chee-*bah*-ooh; a T-shirt with a Brazilian soccer team logo)

In Brazil, you may find tons of knickknacks made from

- **barro** (*bah*-hoh; clay)
- **madeira** (mah-*day*-dah; wood)
- **pedra** (*peh*-drah; stone)
- **palha** (pahl-*yah;* straw)
- **cerâmica** (seh-*dah*-mee-kah; ceramics)

- ✔ **vidro** (*vee*-droh; glass)
- ✔ **semente** (seh-*mehn*-chee; seeds)
- ✔ **renda** (*hehn*-dah; crocheted yarn)

If you want to know whether the item is *handmade*, ask whether it's **feito à mão** (*fay*-toh ah *mah*-ooh). If it's food, the term for *homemade* is **caseiro** (kah-*zay*-doh) — which comes from the word **casa** (*kah*-zah; house).

Shopping for Food and Necessities at the Market

Brazilians shop at **supermercados** (*soo*-peh-meh-*kah*-dooz; supermarkets), but they also love to buy **frutas** (*fdoo*-tahz; fruits) and **legumes e verduras** (leh-*goo*-meez ee veh-*doo*-dahz; vegetables) at **feirinhas** (fay-*deen*-yahz; outdoor markets), where the food is usually **mais barato** (may-eez bah-*dah*-toh; cheaper) and **melhor** (mehl-*yoh;* better).

Getting some practical items

Here are some items you can buy at a **supermercado** (*soo*-peh-meh-*kah*-doo; supermarket), besides **comida** (koh-*mee*-dah; food):

- ✔ **papel higiênico** (pah-*peh*-ooh ee-*zheh*-nee-koh; toilet paper)
- ✔ **produtos de limpeza** (pdoh-*doo*-tohz jee leem-*peh*-zah; cleaning products)
- ✔ **latas de legumes** (*lah*-tahz jee leh-*goo*-meez; cans of vegetables)
- ✔ **coisas congeladas** (*koy*-zahz kohn-zhe-*lah*-dahz; frozen things)
- ✔ **adoçante** (ah-doh-*sahn*-chee; sugar substitute in liquid form — it's very popular in Brazil)
- ✔ **revistas** (heh-*vee*-stahz; magazines)

- **massas** (*mah*-sahz; pasta)
- **temperos** (tehm-*peh*-dooz; herbs and spices)
- **creme dental** (*kdeh*-mee dehn-*tah*-ooh; toothpaste)
- **escova dental** (eh-*skoh*-vah dehn-*tah*-ooh; toothbrush)
- **sabonete** (sah-boh-*neh*-chee; soap)
- **xampu** (shahm-*poo;* shampoo)
- **fralda** (*fdah*-ooh-dah; diapers)
- **aparelho de barbear** (ah-pah-*dehl*-yoh jee bah-bee-*ah;* shaving razor)

Check out www.paodeacucar.com.br to learn the names of more supermarket items in Portuguese.

Shopping at the outdoor market

Now check out the **feirinha** (fay-*deen*-yah; outdoor market). Here are some typical **verduras** (veh-*dooh*-dahz; leafy veggies) and **legumes** (leh-*goo*-meez; veggies that grow underground) you can find:

- **batatas** (bah-*tah*-tahz; potatoes)
- **couve** (*koh*-ooh-vee; bitter greens — necessary to make **feijoada** [fay-zhoh-*ah*-dah; bean/pig-parts stew]; the **couve** is fried with garlic and eaten on the side)
- **coentro** (koh-*ehn*-tdoh; cilantro)
- **salsinha** (sah-ooh-*seen*-yah; parsley)
- **feijão** (fay-*zhow;* beans)
- **pepino** (peh-*pee*-noh; cucumber)
- **brócolis** (*bdoh*-koh-leez; broccoli)
- **espinafre** (ehs-pee-*nah*-fdee; spinach)
- **repolho** (heh-*pol*-yoh; cabbage)
- **berinjela** (beh-dang-*zheh*-lah; eggplant)
- **abóbora** (ah-*boh*-boh-dah; pumpkin)

Here are some types of fish and meat:

- **peixe** (*pay*-shee; fish)
- **frutos do mar** (*fdoo*-tohz doo *mah;* shellfish. *Literally:* fruits of the sea)
- **atum** (ah-*toong;* tuna)
- **salmão** (sah-ooh-*mah*-ooh; salmon)
- **camarões** (kah-mah-*doh*-eez; shrimp)
- **caranguejo** (kahn-*gdeh*-zhoh; crab)
- **lula** (*loo*-lah; squid)
- **polvo** (*pohl*-voh; octopus)
- **cortes de carne** (*koh*-cheez jee *kah*-nee; cuts of meat)
- **carne moída** (*kah*-nee moh-*ee*-dah; ground beef)
- **aves** (*ah*-veez; poultry)
- **frango sem osso** (*fdahn*-goh sang *oh*-soo; boneless chicken)
- **frango com osso** (*fdahn*-goh koh-oong *oh*-soo; boned chicken)

Sometimes the butcher asks whether you want your meat **de primeira ou de segunda** (jee pdee-*may*-dah ooh jee seh-*goon*-dah; Grade A or Grade B).

Making Comparisons and Expressing Opinions

If you're shopping with an **amigo** (ah-*mee*-goh; friend), you may want to share your **opinião** (oh-pee-nee-*ah*-ooh; opinion) about the things in the **loja** (*loh*-zhah; shop).

If you think something is so-so, you can say:

- **Gosto.** (*gohs*-too; I like it.)
- **Está bem.** (eh-*stah bang;* It's okay.)

✔ **Nao está mau.** (*nah*-ooh eh-*stah mah*-ooh; It's not bad.)

Then if you see something that you like even more, you can say:

✔ **Este é melhor.** (*ehs*-chee *eh* meh-ooh-*yoh;* This one's better.)

✔ **Este eu gosto mais.** (*ehs*-chee ee-ooh *goh*-stoo *mah*-eez; I like this one more.)

✔ **É bem bonito este.** (eh *bang* boo-*nee*-too *ehs*-chee; This one's really nice.)

When you see the best one, you can say:

✔ **Este é o melhor.** (ehs-chee eh ooh meh-ooh-yoh; This one's the best.)

✔ **É perfeito este.** (eh peh-*fay*-toh *esh*-chee; This one's perfect.)

Better is **melhor** (meh-ooh-*yoh*), and *the best* is **o melhor** (ooh meh-ooh-*yoh*).

Now comes the fun part. In Portuguese, adding the ending **-ísimo/a** or **-érrimo/a** to the end of some adjectives exaggerates whatever's being said. Something that's nice but not really **caro** (*kah*-doh; expensive) is suddenly **chiquérrimo** (shee-*keh*-hee-moh; really glamorous). Here are some common expressions you can use while shopping:

✔ **Chiquérrimo!** (shee-*keh*-hee-moh! Really glamorous/expensive-looking! — from the word **chique**)

✔ **Caríssimo!** (kah-*dee*-see-moh; So expensive! — from the word **caro**)

Paying for Your Purchases

Here are three of the more common ways of asking how much something is:

✔ **Quanto vale?** (*kwahn*-toh *vah*-lee; How much does it cost? *Literally:* How much is it worth?)

✔ **Quanto custa?** (*kwahn*-toh *koo*-stah; How much does it cost?)

✔ **Quanto é?** (*kwahn*-toh *eh;* How much is it?)

Here's how the vendor usually answers:

✔ **Vale . . . reais.** (*vah*-lee . . . heh-*eyez;* It costs . . . [number] reais.)

✔ **Custa . . . reais.** (*koos*-tah . . . heh-*eyez;* It costs . . . [number] reais.)

✔ **São . . . reais.** (*sah*-ooh . . . heh-*eyez;* It costs . . . [number] reais.)

Luckily, when you **pagar** (pah-*gah;* pay), visible **números** (*noo*-meh-dohz) are often involved. At a nice shop or supermarket, you'll be seeing the number pop up on a cash register. That makes communication a little easier. If you're having problems communicating at an informal, outdoor market (where you often won't find even a calculator), you can always pull out a pen and paper to clear things up.

Here are some other helpful uses of **pagar:**

✔ **Quer pagar agora ou depois?** (*keh* pah-*gah* ah-*goh*-dah ooh deh-*poh*-eez; Do you want to pay now or later?)

✔ **Já pagou?** (zhah pah-*goh;* Did you pay already?)

✔ **Paguei vinte reais.** (pah-*gay veen*-chee heh-*eyez;* I paid 20 reais.)

✔ **Vão pagar a conta.** (*vah*-ooh pah-*gah* ah *kohn*-tah; They will pay the bill.)

These phrases may come in handy when you're at the **caixa** (*kah*-ee-shah; register):

✔ **Tem desconto para estudantes?** (*tang* dehs-*kohn*-toh *pah*-dah eh-stoo-*dahn*-cheez; Do you have a student discount?)

- ✔ **Tem caneta?** (*tang* kah-*neh*-tah; Do you have a pen?)

- ✔ **Me dá um recibo, por favor?** (mee *dah* oong heh-*see*-boh poh fah-*voh;* Can you give me a receipt, please?)

The vendor may ask you:

- ✔ **Tem algum documento? Um passaporte?** (*tang* ah-ooh-*goong* doh-koo-*mehn*-toh oong pah-sah-*poh*-chee; Do you have some I.D.? A passport?)

- ✔ **Qual é a validade do cartão?** (*kwah*-ooh *eh* ah vah-lee-*dah*-jee doo kah-*tah*-ooh; What's the expiration on the card?)

As a rule of thumb, you can bargain in Brazil in outdoor **mercados** (meh-*kah*-dooz; markets) but not inside **lojas** (*loh*-zhahz; stores). At **feirinhas** (fay-*deen*-yahz; outdoor food markets), most locals don't bargain, though you can always try — it won't be considered offensive.

Start out by asking how much something costs, and then offer a lower price or tell the vendor you have only a certain amount of money:

- ✔ **Quanto custa?** (*kwahn*-toh *koo*-stah; How much does it cost?)

- ✔ **Quanto é?** (*kwahn*-toh *eh;* How much is it?)

- ✔ **Posso pagar . . . reais?** (*pah*-sooh pah-*gah* . . . heh-*eyez;* Can I pay . . . [number] reais?)

- ✔ **Só tenho vinte reais.** (*soh tang*-yoh *veen*-chee heh-*eyez;* I have only twenty reais.)

You can then accept the price the vendor gives you or make a final offer.

Of course, if you tell the vendor you only have 15 reais, you probably don't want to pay with a 20-real bill. Separate the bills you want to use to pay for the item before approaching the stall.

Chapter 7

Making Leisure a Top Priority

. . . .

In This Chapter

▶ Asking about an event and giving and receiving invitations

▶ Going out on the town

▶ Taking in some music

▶ Exploring museums, movies, and special events

▶ Going to the beach

▶ Talking about soccer and other forms of recreation

▶ Talking about love

. . . .

*B*razil is probably most famous for its **praias** (*pdah*-ee-ahz; beaches) and **Carnaval** (kah-nah-*vah*-ooh). But that's not all that Brazilian culture is. The country has fabulous **museus** (moo-*zay*-ooz; museums), a vibrant arts scene, and **música ao vivo** (*moo*-zee-*kah* ah-ooh *vee*-voo; live music).

This chapter tells you what you need to know to explore and appreciate the art and culture of Brazil and to enjoy yourself as much as any Brazilian.

Talking about Going Out

Tem vontade de sair? (tang vohn-*tah*-jee jee sah-*eeh;* Are you in the mood to go out?).

Whether you're itching for **música ao vivo** (*moo*-zee-*kah* ah-ooh *vee*-voo; live music) or something else, you can use the following phrase to ask locals what you can do around town: **O que recomenda para fazer hoje à noite?** (ooh *keh* heh-koh-*mehn*-dah pah-dah fah-*zeh* oh-zhee ah *noh*-ee-chee; What do you recommend doing tonight?).

The locals will probably then ask you **De/do que você gosta?** (jee/dooh *keh* voh-*seh* goh-stah; What do you like?). You can respond **Gosto de . . .** (*goh*-stoh *jee;* I like . . .)

- ✔ **bares** (*bah*-deez; bars)
- ✔ **boates** (boh-*ah*-cheez; nightclubs)
- ✔ **espetáculos** (eh-speh-*tah*-koo-lohz; shows)
- ✔ **eventos culturais** (eh-*vehn*-tohz kool-too-*dah*-eez; cultural events)
- ✔ **cinema** (see-*neh*-mah; cinema)
- ✔ **teatro** (chee-*ah*-tdoh; theater)
- ✔ **festas** (*fehs*-tahz; parties)

If you're new in town and just want to ask how to get to the **centro** (*sehn*-tdoh; downtown), say **Onde fica o centro?** (*ohn*-jee *fee*-kah ooh *sehn*-tdoh; Where's the downtown area?).

Inviting someone and being invited

If you want to invite someone out on the town with you, you can say one of the following:

- ✔ **Quer ir comigo?** (*keh* ee koh-*mee*-goh; Do you want to go with me?)

✔ **Quer vir conosco?** (*keh vee* koh-*noh*-skoh;
Do you want to come with us?)

✔ **Quero te convidar.** (*keh*-doo chee kohn-vee-*dah;*
I want to invite you.)

✔ **Estou te convidando!** (eh-*stoh* chee kohn-vee-
dahn-doh; I'm inviting you!)

✔ **Vem conosco!** (*vang* koh-*noh*-skoh; Come
with us!)

✔ **Vem comigo!** (*vang* koh-*mee*-goh; Come
with me!)

Here are some more-specific examples of common
expressions using **convidar** (kohn-vee-*dah;* to invite):

✔ **Quero convidar a todos para a minha casa.**
(*keh*-doo kohn-vee-*dah* ah *toh*-dooz *pah*-dah ah
meen-yah *kah*-zah; I want to invite everyone to
my house.)

✔ **Estão convidando a gente para ir à praia.** (eh-
stah-ooh kohn-vee-*dahn*-doh ah *zhang*-chee pah-
dah eeh ah *pdah*-ee-ah; They're inviting us to go
to the beach.)

Brazilians often say **a gente** (ah *zhang*-chee)
rather than **nós** (nohz) to mean "we" or "us."
A gente literally means "the people." Strange
but true, and fun to say.

Asking what the place or event is like

To get more details about an **evento** (eh-*vehn*-toh;
event) or **lugar** (loo-*gah;* place), you may want to ask
for **mais detalhes** (*mah*-eez deh-*tahl*-yeez; more
details). Here are the what, when, how, where, and
why questions:

✔ **Como é o lugar?** (koh-moh *eh* ooh loo-*gah;*
What's the place like?)

✔ **Quando começa?** (*kwahn*-doh koh-*meh*-sah;
When does it start?)

✔ **Onde fica?** (*ohn*-jee *fee*-kah; Where is it?)

✔ **Tem algum motivo?** (*tang* ah-ooh-goong moh-*chee*-voh; Why is it being put on?)

✔ **O que é, exatamente?** (ooh kee eh, eh-zah-tah-*mehn*-chee; What is it, exactly?)

And check out some additional phrases that can give you even more clues about what to do:

✔ **Custa caro?** (*koo*-stah *kah*-doh; Is it expensive?)

✔ **Vai ter muitas pessoas?** (*vah*-ee *teh* moh-*ee*-tahz peh-*soh*-ahz; Will there be a lot of people?)

✔ **Que tipo de música vai ter?** (kee *chee*-poh jee *moo*-zee-kah vah-ee *teh;* What type of music will there be?)

✔ **Que tipo de gente?** (kee *chee*-poh jee *zhang*-chee; What type of people?)

✔ **É informal ou formal?** (eh een-foh-*mah*-ooh ooh foh-*mah*-ooh; Is it informal or formal?)

✔ **Vale a pena ir?** (*vah*-lee ah *peh*-nah *ee;* Is it worth going to?)

Here are some answers you're likely to get about an event:

✔ **Não custa caro.** (*nah*-ooh *koo*-stah *kah*-doh; It's not expensive.)

✔ **Vai ser muito bom.** (*vah*-ee *seh* moh-*ee*-toh *boh*-oong; It's going to be really good.)

✔ **Vale a pena.** (*vah*-lee ah *peh*-nah; It's worth going to.)

✔ **Deve ter bastante gente.** (deh-vee *teh* bah-*stahn*-chee *zhang*-chee; There should be a lot of people.)

✔ **O lugar é pequeno.** (ooh loo-*gah* eh peh-*keh*-noh; The place is small.)

✔ **É muito jovem.** (*eh* moh-*ee*-toh *zhoh*-vang; It's really young.)

✔ **É para todas as idades.** (*eh pah*-dah *toh*-dahz ahz ee-*dah*-jeez; It's for all ages.)

✔ **É um bar gay.** (*eh* oong *bah gay;* It's a gay bar.)

You will also hear a "gay" place described as GLS (zeh eh-lee eh-see), or gay, **lésbicas e simpatizantes** (gay, lehz-bee-kahs ee seem-pah-chee-zahn-cheez; gay, lesbian, and those sympathetic). Brazilians say both "gay" and "GLS."

Two other important questions to ask in Brazil about bars or events is whether there's an **entrada** (ehn-*tdah*-dah; cover charge) and whether the place has a **con-sumação mínima** (kohn-soo-mah-*sah*-ooh *mee*-nee-mah; dollar-amount minimum), meaning you'd perhaps have to consume at least $10, say, in drinks or food. Ask **Tem entrada?** (*tang* ehn-*tdah*-dah; Does it have a cover charge?) or **Tem consumação mínima?** (*tang* kohn-soo-mah-*sah*-ooh *mee*-nee-mah; Is there a minimum?).

Asking People What They Like to Do

As you make friends, you want to know what hobbies or interests you have in common. Just say **Você gosta de . . . ?** (voh-seh *goh*-stah jee; Do you like . . . ?) and then add in the activity, like this:

✔ **Você gosta de surfar?** (voh-seh *goh*-stah jee soo-*fah;* Do you like to surf?)

✔ **Você gosta de ir à academia?** (voh-*seh goh*-stah jee *ee* ah ah-kah-deh-*mee*-ah; Do you like to go to the gym?)

✔ **Você gosta de correr?** (voh-*seh goh*-stah jee koh-*heh;* Do you like to go running?)

✔ **Você gosta de jogar futebol?** (voh-*seh goh*-stah jee zhoh-*gah* foo-chee-*bah*-ooh; Do you like to play soccer?)

If someone asks you one of these questions, you can answer **Sim, gosto** (*sing goh*-stoo; Yeah, I like it) or **Não, não gosto** (*nah*-ooh, *nah*-ooh *goh*-stoo; No, I don't like it).

You can use the **você gosta de . . .** formula for a ton of fun activities, like these:

- ✔ **Você gosta de viajar?** (voh-seh *goh*-stah jee vee-ah-*zhah;* Do you like to travel?)

- ✔ **Você gosta de ir ao cinema?** (voh-*seh goh*-stah jee *ee* ah-ooh see-*neh*-mah; Do you like to go to the movies?)

- ✔ **Você gosta de praticar o seu inglês?** (voh-*seh goh*-stah jee pdah-chee-*kah* ooh seh-ooh eeng-*glehz;* Do you like practicing your English?)

- ✔ **Você gosta de cozinhar?** (voh-*seh goh*-stah jee koh-zeeng-*yah;* Do you like to cook?)

Expressing your most passionate feelings in another language is always difficult. But here are a couple of easy tricks: To say you love doing something, use **Eu adoro . . .** (eh-ooh ah-*doh*-doo; I love . . .). If you hate it, say **Eu detesto . . .** (eh-ooh deh-*tehs*-toh; I hate . . .).

Taking in Brazil's Musical Culture

The one thing you shouldn't miss doing in Brazil **de noite** (*jee noh*-ee-chee; at night) is listening to **música ao vivo** (*moo*-zee-kah ah-ooh *vee*-voh; live music). Or pick up an instrument and play yourself!

Playing an instrument

Você toca algum instrumento? (voh-*seh toh*-kah ah-ooh-*goong* een-stdoo-*mehn*-toh; Do you play an instrument?). In Brazil, the **violão** (vee-ooh-*lah*-ooh; guitar) is by far the most common instrument played. But Brazilians appreciate all kinds of music, and anything having to do with music is a great conversation starter.

Take a glance at some names of instruments in Portuguese:

- ✔ **o violão** (ooh vee-ooh-*lah*-ooh; acoustic guitar)
- ✔ **a guitarra** (ah gee-tah-hah; electric guitar)
- ✔ **a bateria** (ah *bah*-teh-*dee*-ah; drums)
- ✔ **o baixo** (ooh *bah*-ee-shoh; bass guitar)
- ✔ **a flauta** (ah *flah*-ooh-tah; flute)
- ✔ **o piano** (ooh pee-*ah*-noh; piano)
- ✔ **o violino** (ooh vee-oh-*lee*-noh; violin)

Now for the Brazilian instruments. Perhaps hundreds of instruments are specific to Brazil and Brazilian music. Music is Brazilians' artistic specialty, after all. Here are some of the most famous ones:

- ✔ **a cuíca** (ah *kwee*-kah; a stick that's rubbed through what looks like a small drum — it makes a donkey hee-haw or whine, depending on how it's moved)
- ✔ **o berimbau** (ooh *beh*-deem-*bah*-ooh; a large bow that's played with a wooden stick — it's used to accompany the Brazilian martial arts form **capoeira** [kay-poh-*ay*-dah])
- ✔ **o paxixi** (ooh pah-shee-*shee;* a woven rattle)
- ✔ **o cavaquinho** (ooh kah-vah-*keen*-yoh; an instrument similar to a ukulele — it's used in bands that play **forró** music, which originates in the northeast and sounds similar to country)
- ✔ **o pandeiro** (ooh pahn-*day*-doh; a tambourine)
- ✔ **a sanfona** (ah sahn-*foh*-nah; an accordion — used for **forró** music)

And here are some phrases about playing these instruments:

✔ **Eu toco piano.** (*eh*-ooh *toh*-koo pee-*ah*-noh; I play the piano.)

✔ **Ela toco bateria.** (*eh*-lah *toh*-kah bah-teh-*dee*-ah; She plays the drums.)

✔ **Eles tocam violão.** (*eh*-leez *toh*-kah-ooh vee-oh-*lah*-ooh; They play the guitar.)

Brazilians use the guitar as the model of the ideal woman's body. English-speakers say "hourglass figure"; Brazilians say **corpo de violão** (*koh*-poo jee vee-ooh-*lah*-ooh; guitar-shaped body).

Dancing around and singing out loud

Especially if you're **solteiro** (sohl-*tay*-doh; a single person), you'll probably want to learn how to ask someone to **dançar** (dahn-*sah;* dance) and how you'll be asked to **dançar**.

Couple-dancing is very common in Brazil. The most popular form is probably **forró** (foh-*hah*), a fast-paced country-sounding music and accompanying dance form that originates in the northeast. **Samba** (*sahm*-bah), the best-known music and dance from Brazil, is generally not for **casais** (kah-*zah*-eez; couples), at least during festivals. You dance **sozinho** (soh-*zeen*-yoh; alone).

Here are some common expressions that use **dançar:**

✔ **Vamos dançar?** (*vah*-mohz dahn-*sah;* Shall we dance?)

✔ **Quer dançar comigo?** (keh dahn-*sah* koh-*mee*-goh; Do you want to dance with me?)

✔ **Não sei dançar.** (*nah*-ooh *say* dahn-*sah;* I don't know how to dance.)

Você gosta de cantar? (voh-*seh goh*-stah jee kahn-*tah;* Do you like to sing?). Here are some ways you can use **cantar:**

- ✔ **Ela canta super bem.** (eh-lah *kahn*-tah *soo*-peh *bang;* She sings really well.)

- ✔ **Eu não canto muito bem.** (*eh*-ooh *nah*-ooh *kahn*-toh moh-*ee*-toh *bang;* I don't sing very well.)

- ✔ **Você canta? Não sabia.** (voh-*seh kahn*-tah *nah*-ooh sah-*bee*-ah; You sing? I didn't know.)

- ✔ **Nós cantamos no chuveiro.** (nohz kahn-*tah*-mohz noh shoo-*vay*-doh; We sing in the shower.)

Exploring Carnaval in Brazil

Brazil is world-famous for its **Carnaval** (kah-nah-*vah*-ooh; Carnival). The festivities take place usually in **fevereiro** (feh-veh-*day*-doh; February) or **março** (*mah*-soo; March), when the weather is hot in Brazil, for the four days preceding **Quarta-feira de Cinzas** (*kwah*-tah-*fay*-dah jee *seen*-zahz; Ash Wednesday).

Every Brazilian has a different opinion on which Carnaval is best. Here are some questions you can ask a Brazilian to help you decide which Carnaval is right for you:

- ✔ **Qual Carnaval no Brasil você acha melhor?** (*kwah*-ooh kah-nah-*vah*-ooh noh bdah-*zee*-ooh *ah*-shah mel-*yoh;* Which Carnaval in Brazil do you think is best?)

- ✔ **Qual é o mais divertido?** (*kwah*-ooh *eh* ooh *mah*-eez jee-veh-*chee*-doo; Which one is the most fun?)

- ✔ **Qual tem o melhor show?** (*kwah*-ooh *tang* ah mel-*yoh shoh;* Which one has the best show?)

- ✔ **Qual tem o melhor carnaval de rua?** (*kwah*-ooh *tang* oh mel-*yoh* kah-nah-*vah*-ooh jee *hoo*-ah; Which one has the best street carnival?)

- ✔ **Já esteve no Carnaval de . . . ?** (*zhah* eh-*steh*-vee noo kah-nah-*vah*-ooh jee; Have you been to the Carnaval in . . . ?)

Exploring Art Galleries and Museums

Brazil has plenty of **galerias de arte** (gah-leh-*dee*-ahz jee *ah*-chee; art galleries), **centros culturais** (*sehn*-tdohz kool-too-*dah*-eez; cultural centers), and **museus** (moo-*zeh*-oohz; museums). The biggest and most famous ones are in some of the country's largest cities: São Paulo, Brasilia, and Rio.

Here are some things you'll find in a gallery or museum:

- **exibições temporárias** (*eggs*-ee-bee-*soy*-eez temp-oh-*dah*-dee-ahz; temporary exhibitions)
- **quadros** (*kwah*-drohz; paintings)
- **esculturas** (eh-skool-*too*-dahz; sculptures)
- **fotografias** (foh-toh-gdah-*fee*-ahz; photographs)
- **objetos históricos** (ohb-*zheh*-tohz ee-*stoh*-dee-kohz; historic objects)

Check out some phrases that deal with **a arte** (ah *ah*-chee; art):

- **Você gosta de arte?** (voh-*seh goh*-stah jee *ah*-chee; Do you like art?)
- **Tem uma exibição muito boa no Itaú Cultural.** (*tang ooh*-mah eggs-ee-bee-*sah*-ooh moh-*ee*-toh *boh*-ah noh ee-tah-*ooh* kool-too-*dah*-ooh; There's a really good exhibition at Itaú Cultural Center.)
- **Tem uns quadros famosos do Picasso naquele museu.** (*tang* oonz *kwah*-drohz fah-*moh*-zooz doo pee-*kah*-soh nah-*keh*-lee moo-*zeh*-ooh; There are some famous Picasso paintings in that museum.)
- **Eu adoro as vernissages.** (*ee*-ooh ah-*doh*-doo ahz veh-nee-*sah*-zhehz; I love art exhibition opening nights.)

Going to the Movies

What type of **filmes** (*fee*-ooh-meez; movies) do you like? Have you ever seen **um filme brasileiro** (oong *fee*-ooh-mee bdah-zee-*lay*-doh; a Brazilian movie)? You may be surprised to find out that the Brazilian **indústria de filmes** (een-*doo*-stee-ah jee *fee*-ooh-meez; film industry) is very large and of high quality.

At most **salas de cinema** (*sah*-lahz jee see-*neh*-mah; movie theaters) in Brazil, about half of the **filmes** playing are Brazilian — several **filmes novos** (*fee*-ooh-meez *noh*-vooz; new films) come out every month. You may want to ask whether the movie is **legendado** (leh-zhang-*dah*-doo; subtitled) or **dublado** (doo-*blah*-doo; dubbed over). Subtitled films are also sometimes referred to as **versão original** (veh-*sah*-ooh oh-*dee*-zhee-*nah*-ooh; original version).

Here are some handy phrases you can use to talk about **filmes**:

- ✔ **Vamos ao cinema?** (*vah*-mohz ah-ooh see-*neh*-mah; Do you want to go to the movies?)

- ✔ **Quer assistir um filme?** (*keh* ah-sees-*chee* oong *fee*-ooh-mee; Do you want to see a movie?)

- ✔ **De que tipo de filmes gosta?** (Jee kee *chee*-poh jee *fee*-ooh-meez *goh*-stah; What type of movies do you like?)

- ✔ **Estou com vontade de assistir uma comédia.** (eh-*stoh koh*-oong vohn-*tah*-jee jee ah-sees-*chee* ooh-mah koh-*meh*-jah; I feel like seeing a comedy.)

- ✔ **Você espera na fila, e eu compro a pipoca.** (voh-*seh* eh-*speh*-dah nah *fee*-lah, ee *eh*-ooh *kohm*-pdoh ah pee-*poh*-kah; You wait in the line, and I'll buy the popcorn.)

- ✔ **Qual filme gostaria de ver?** (*kwah*-ooh *fee*-ooh-mee gohs-tah-*dee*-ah jee *veh;* Which movie would you like to see?)

Words to Know

Estou com vontade . . .	eh-<u>stoh</u> kohng vohn-<u>tah</u>-jee	I feel like . . . (what you feel like doing)
assistir	ah-sees-<u>chee</u>	to see (a movie, a show, TV)
uma comédia	<u>ooh</u>-mah koh-<u>meh</u>-jah	a comedy
fila	<u>fee</u>-lah	line (of people)
bom	<u>boh</u>-oong	so/well
vamos	<u>vah</u>-mohz	let's go/should we go?
espera	eh-<u>speh</u>-dah	wait
pipoca	pee-<u>poh</u>-kah	popcorn
Acha . . . ?	<u>ah</u>-shah	Do you think . . . ?

Names of non-Brazilian **filmes,** like American or European ones, are often translated slightly differently into Portuguese — and often with a funny result. My favorite is the movie *O Brother, Where Art Thou?* (2000), which was translated as **E Aí, Irmão, Cadê Você?** (ee ah-*ee* eeh-*mah*-ooh kah-*deh* voh-*seh*; Hey, Dude, Where Are You?).

Hanging Out at the Beach

Most of Brazil's population is concentrated near its **litoral** (lee-toh-*dah*-oo; coastline), making **praias** (*pdah*-ee-ahz; beaches) a focus of daily life for many locals.

It's an opportunity to sip **água de coco** (ah-gwah jee *koh*-koh; coconut water, sipped through a straw, out of a green coconut) or drink a **cerveja** (seh-*veh*-zhah; beer) with old friends and a chance to make new acquaintances, too. At urban beaches, you may see many people **fazendo cooper** (fah-*zen*-doh *koo*-peh; jogging) on the beachfront avenue and some **surfistas** (soo-*fee*-stahs; surfers).

What to take to the beach

It's a myth that all Brazilian **mulheres** (moo-*yeh*-deez; women) wear itsy-bitsy, teeny-weeny, thong bikini bottoms. In Portuguese, thong bikini bottoms are called **fio dental** (*fee*-oh dang-*tah*-ooh; dental floss) — Brazilians always have a sense of humor. It is true, however, that the average top and bottom parts of a Brazilian **biquíni** (bee-*kee*-nee; bikini) are **menor** (meh-*noh;* smaller) than the average American or European bikini.

Here are some items that you're sure to see people wearing on a beach:

- **sungas** (*soong*-gahz; Speedo-style swim trunks)
- **bermudas** (beh-*moo*-dahz; longer, American-style swimming shorts — Bermuda shorts)
- **chinelos** (shee-*neh*-looz; flip-flops)
- **toalha** (toe-*ahl*-yah; towel)
- **canga** (*kang*-gah; sarong to sit down on)
- **óculos de sol** (oh-koo-lohz jee *soh*-oo; sunglasses)
- **protetor solar** (pdoh-teh-*toh* soh-*lah;* sunblock)

Check out what else you will find on a beach:

- **barraca** (bah-*hah*-kah; beach shack that serves food/drinks)
- **areia** (ah-*day*-ah; sand)
- **frescobol** (*fdeh*-skoo-*bah*-ooh; beach ping-pong)

✔ **crianças** (kdee-*ahn*-sahz; kids)

✔ **livros** (*leev*-dohz; books)

✔ **pescadores** (pehs-kah-*doh*-deez; fishermen)

✔ **futebol** (foo-chee-*bah*-ooh; soccer)

✔ **vôlei** (*voh*-lay; volleyball)

✔ **cadeira de praia** (kah-*deh*-dah jee *pdah*-ee-ah; beach chair)

✔ **sombrinha** (sohm-*bdeen*-yah; beach umbrella. *Literally:* little shade)

✔ **prancha de surf** (*pdahn*-shah jee *sooh*-fee; surfboard)

You can also buy snacks, which generally cost **um real** (oong heh-*ah*-ooh; one Brazilian real, or about 35 cents). People walk by, shouting **Um real! Um real!** with the name of the food they're selling. Typical beach snack food includes

✔ **queijo coalho** (*kay*-zhoh koh-*ahl*-yoh; barbequed cheese cubes)

✔ **um espeto de carne** (oong eh-*speh*-toh jee *kah*-nee; a beef shish kabob)

✔ **amendoim** (ah-*mang*-doh-*eeng;* peanuts)

✔ **picolé** (pee-koh-*leh;* fruity popsicles)

Here's a conversation you might have when getting ready for the beach:

Paula: **Temos protetor solar?** (teh-mohz pdoh-teh-*toh* soh-*lah?* Do we have sunblock?)

Rogério: **Sim, mas só fator oito. Tá bom para ti (ok)?** (sing, *maz soh* fah-*toh* oh-ee-toh. tah *boh-oong* pah-dah *chee*? Yeah, but it's just SPF 8. Is that okay for you?)

Paula: **Sim, tá bom. Eu estou com uma canga, mas acho suficiente para os dois.** (sing, tah *boh-oong*. *eh*-ooh ehs-*toh* kohng ooh-mah *kahng*-gah, maz *ah*-shoo soo-fee-see-*ehn*-chee pah-dah ooze *doh*-eez; Yeah, that's fine. I have one sarong [to lay down on], but I think it's enough for the two of us.)

Rogério: **Ótimo. Agora só quero uma cerveja.** (*oh*-chee-moh. ah-*goh*-dah soh keh-doo ooh-mah seh-*veh*-zhah; Great. Now I just want a beer.)

Paula: **Eu estou de regime. Vou tomar uma água de coco.** (*eh*-ooh ehs-*toh* jee heh-*zhee*-mee. voh toh-*mah* oo-mah ah-gwah jee *koh*-koo; I'm on a diet. I'm going to have coconut water.)

Words to Know

Temos . . . ?	<u>teh</u>-mohz	Do we have . . . ?
fator . . .	fah-<u>toh</u>	SPF . . . number
para ti	pah-dah <u>chee</u>	for you
Tá bom.	tah <u>boh-oong</u>	That's fine.
acho	<u>ah</u>-shoo	I think
Ótimo	<u>oh</u>-chee-moh	Great.
agora	ah-<u>goh</u>-dah	now
regime	heh-<u>zhee</u>-mee	diet

Talking about beach safety

Beaches are for relaxing. But before settling into your chair and making grooves into the sand, it's always best to ask some basic **perguntas** (peh-*goon*-tahz; questions) that concern your **segurança** (seh-goo-*dahn*-sah; safety). Check out some useful phrases about beach safety:

- ✔ **Tem ladrão aqui?** (tang lah-*drah*-ooh ah-*kee;* Are there pickpockets around here?)

- ✔ **É perigosa a ressaca aqui?** (eh peh-dee-*goh*-zoo ah heh-*sah*-kah ah-*kee;* Is the undercurrent strong here?)

- ✔ **Tem salva-vida aqui?** (tang *sah*-oo-vah *vee*-dah ah-*kee;* Are there any lifeguards here?)

- ✔ **Tem tubarão aqui?** (tang too-bah-*dah*-ooh ah-*kee;* Are there sharks here?)

- ✔ **A praia tem pedras?** (ah *pdah*-ee-ah tang *peh*-drahz; Is the beach rocky?)

And here are some responses you may get:

- ✔ **Sim, é perigoso.** (*sing* eh peh-dee-*goh*-zoo; Yes, it's dangerous.)

- ✔ **Sim, cuidado.** (sing, kwee-*dah*-doh; Yes, be careful/watch out.)

- ✔ **Não se preocupe.** (nah-ooh see pdeh-oh-*koo*-pee; Don't worry.)

- ✔ **Não, é tranqüilo.** (nah-ooh eh tdahn-*kwee*-loo; No, it's safe.)

Yell **Socorro!** (soh-*koh*-hoo; Help!) if you're in immediate danger.

On urban beaches, flags stuck in the sand often say **Perigoso** (peh-dee-*goh*-zoo; Dangerous) to alert you that entering the water is unsafe.

Expressing beauty: "It's so beautiful!"

All beaches have a unique beauty, of course. Check out some phrases you can use to talk about how pretty a beach is:

- ✔ **Que bonita!** (kee boh-*nee*-tah; How pretty!)

- ✔ **É maravilhosa!** (eh mah-dah-vee-lee-*oh*-zah; It's amazing!)

✔ **Incrível!** (eeng-*kdee*-veh-ooh; Unbelievable!)

✔ **Nossa senhora!** (noh-sah seen-*yoh*-dah; Wow!)

✔ **Que legal!** (kee leh-*gah*-ooh; How cool!)

✔ **Meu Deus!** (meh-oo *deh*-ooz; Oh my God!)

✔ **Não acredito!** (*nah*-ooh ah-kdeh-*jee*-toh; I can't believe it!)

> **Nossa senhora!** literally means "Our lady" and would be the English equivalent of saying, "Holy Mary, mother of God!" It's very common in Brazil, and people often just say **Nossa!**

Getting Out for a Walk (or a Hike)

Taking **uma caminhada** (ooh-mah kah-meen-*yah*-dah; a walk) along the **beira-mar** (bay-dah-*mah;* seashore) is one of life's simple pleasures. In Brazil, you'll see many people walking along the beach — in order to **se divertir** (see jee-veh-*chee;* enjoy themselves), to **observar as pessoas** (ohb-seh-*vah* ahz peh-*soh*-az; people-watch), and for **exercício** (eh-seh-*see*-see-ooh; exercise).

On **praias urbanas** (*pdah*-ee-ahz ooh-*bahn*-az; urban beaches), people especially like to walk on the **calçadão** (cow-sah-*dah*-ooh; broad beachfront sidewalk). In Rio, the sidewalks have a famous black-and-white pattern that look like **ondas** (*ohn*-dahz; waves).

In Brazil's rain forests and **mata atlântica** (mah-tah aht-*lahn*-chee-kah; jungle regions near the coast, in southeast Brazil) people like **fazer trilha** (fah-*zeh* tdeel-yah; to hike).

These phrases can help you talk about walking:

✔ **Eu adoro caminhar pela praia.** (eh-ooh ah-*doh*-doo kah-mee-*yah* peh-lah *pdah*-ee-ah; I love to walk on the beach.)

✔ **Vamos fazer uma caminhada na praia?** (vah-mohz fah-*zeh* ooh-mah kah-mee-*yah*-dah nah *pdah*-ee-ah? Shall we go for a walk on the beach?)

✔ **Eu preciso fazer exercício.** (eh-ooh pdeh-*see*-zoo fah-*zeh* eh-seh-*see*-soo; I need to do exercise.)

✔ **Nós caminhamos pela cidade sempre.** (nohz kah-mee-*yah*-mohz peh-lah see-*dah*-jee *same*-pdee; We always walk around the city.)

✔ **Ela caminha muito devagar.** (eh-lah kah-*mee*-yah moh-*ee*-toh deh-vah-*gah;* She walks really slowly.)

✔ **Ele caminha muito rápido.** (eh-lee kah-*mee*-yah moh-*ee*-toh *hah*-pee-doh; He walks very fast.)

✔ **Eles tem que caminhar até o estacionamento.** (eh-leez *tang* kee kah-mee-*yah* ah-*teh* ooh ehs-*tah*-see-ohn-ah-*mehn*-toh; They have to walk to the parking lot.)

Here are some words associated with hiking and walking:

✔ **trilha** (*tdee*-ooh-yah; trail)

✔ **fazer trilha** (fah-*zeh tdee*-ooh-yah; to hike)

✔ **correr** (koh-*heh;* to run/jog)

✔ **rápido** (*hah*-pee-doh; fast)

✔ **devagar** (deh-vah-*gah;* slow)

✔ **caminho** (kah-*mee*-yo; road)

✔ **conversar** (kohn-veh-*sah;* to chat)

✔ **pensar** (pehn-*sah;* to think)

✔ **relaxar** (heh-lah-*shah;* to relax)

Playing Soccer — Brazil's National Pastime

Futebol (foo-chee-*bah*-ooh; soccer) is a very important topic in Brazil — probably even more important than **religião** (heh-lee-zhee-*ah*-ooh; religion). The fastest way to make an **amigo** (ah-*mee*-goo; friend) — whether it be a Brazilian man or a woman — is to share the same favorite Brazilian soccer team.

Most of Brazil's famous soccer teams are in Rio or São Paulo. Here's a quick rundown of the teams and which cities they're based in:

- **Flamengo** (flah-*mang*-goh): city of Rio
- **Botafogo** (boh-tah-*foh*-goh): city of Rio
- **São Paulo** (sah-ooh *pah*-oo-loh): city of São Paulo
- **Corinthians** (koh-*deen*-chee-ahnz): city of São Paulo
- **Santos** (*sahn*-tohz): beach city in São Paulo state — claim to fame is being Pelé's first professional team

Besides soccer, there are a few other sports that Brazilians like as well:

- **basquete** (bahs-*keh*-chee; basketball)
- **tênis** (*teh*-neez; tennis)
- **vôlei** (*voh*-lay; volleyball)
- **surfe** (*sooh*-fee; surfing)
- **natação** (nah-tah-*sah*-oong; swimming)
- **cooper** (*koo*-peh; jogging)

Check out some words that relate to all forms of exercise and recreation. All lead to **boa saúde** (*boh*-ah sah-*ooh*-jee; good health):

- ✔ **academia** (ah-kah-deh-*mee*-ah; gym)

- ✔ **levantar pesos** (leh-vahn-*tah* peh-zohz; to lift weights)

- ✔ **buggy** (*boo*-gee; sand-dune buggy — common in northeastern Brazil)

- ✔ **jangada** (zhahng-*gah*-dah; tiny sailboat — common in northeastern Brazil)

- ✔ **ir de barco** (ee jee *bah*-koh; to take a boat ride)

- ✔ **fazer snorkeling** (fah-*zeh* snoh-keh-ooh-leeng; to snorkel)

- ✔ **fazer mergulho** (fah-*zeh* meh-*gool*-yoh; to scuba dive)

- ✔ **escalada em rocha** (ehs-kah-*lah*-dah ang *hoh*-shah; rock climbing)

- ✔ **ir de bicicleta** (eed jee bee-see-*kleh*-tah; to go bicycling)

There are a number of places to do **esportes radicais** (eh-*spoh*-cheez hah-jee-*kah*-eez; extreme sports) in Brazil. You can **voar de asa delta** (voh-*ah* jee ah-zah *deh*-ooh-tah; go hang gliding) in Rio, over Ipanema beach.

Falling in Love — in Portuguese

Brazilian Portuguese is an extremely romantic language — not only are the sounds beautiful and melodic, but Brazilians themselves are very **românti-cos** (hoh-*mahn*-chee-kooz; romantic). And you can't separate the **língua** (*ling*-gwah; language) from its **cul-tura** (kool-*too*-dah; culture). The language **está cheia de poesia** (eh-*stah* shay-ah jee poh-eh-*zee*-ah; is full of poetry).

Brazilians even have a specific verb to describe the act of smooching about town with your honey: **namorar** (*nah*-moh-*dah*). The root of the verb is **amor.** What did **Jaqueline** (*zhah*-keh-*lee*-nee) do Saturday?

Ela foi namorar (*eh*-lah *foh*-ee *nah*-moh-*dah;* She hung out with her boyfriend).

Girlfriend, by the way, is **namorada** (nah-moh-*dah*-dah), and boyfriend is **namorado** (nah-moh-*dah*-doo). After things move along and the happy couple has a **casamento** (*kah*-zah-*men*-toh; wedding), they become husband and wife — **marido e mulher** (mah-*dee*-doo ee mool-*yeh*).

Check out some classic romantic phrases in Portuguese:

- ✔ **Eu te amo.** (*eh*-ooh chee *ah*-moo; I love you.)

- ✔ **Voce se casaria comigo?** (voh-*seh* see kah-zah-*dee*-ah koh-*mee*-goo; Will you marry me?)

- ✔ **Eu estou apaixonado/a.** (*eh*-ooh eh-*stoh* ah-pah-ee-shee-ooh-*nah*-doo/dah; I'm in love.)

- ✔ **Estou com muita saudade de você.** (eh-*stoh* kohng moh-*ee*-tah sah-ooh-*dah*-jee jee voh-*seh;* I miss you very much.)

- ✔ **Me dá um beijo.** (mee *dah* oong *bay*-zhoh; Give me a kiss.)

- ✔ **Eu vou te amar por toda a minha vida.** (*eh*-ooh *voh* chee ah-*mah* poh *toh*-dah ah ming-yah *vee*-dah; I'm going to love you for the rest of my life.)

And here's how Brazilians say sweet nothings:

- ✔ **o meu amor** (ooh *meh*-ooh ah-*moh*; my love)

- ✔ **o meu querido/a minha querida** (ooh *meh*-ooh keh-*dee*-doo/ah *ming*-yah keh-*dee*-dah; my honey. *Literally:* my loved one)

- ✔ **o meu fofinho/a minha fofinha** (ooh *meh*-ooh foh-*fing*-yoh/ah *ming*-yah foh-*fing*-yah; my sweetie. *Literally:* my soft, fluffy one)

Here are some classic romantic phrases that Brazilians use to **paquerar** (pah-keh-*dah;* flirt):

✔ **Você é muito lindo/a.** (voh-*seh* eh moh-*ee*-toh *leen*-doh/dah; You're really handsome/ beautiful.)

✔ **Você tem olhos muito bonitos.** (voh-*seh* tang *ohl*-yooz moh-*ee*-toh boo-*nee*-tooz; You have very pretty eyes.)

✔ **Gosto muito de você.** (*goh*-stoo moh-*ee*-toh jee voh-*seh;* I really like you.)

Here are some practical phrases, too, for when you meet someone you're interested in:

✔ **Me dá o seu número de telefone?** (mee *dah* ooh *seh*-ooh *noo*-meh-doh jee teh-leh-*foh*-nee; Will you give me your phone number?)

✔ **O que vai fazer amanhã?** (ooh *kee vah*-ee fah-*zeh* ah-mahn-*yah;* What are you doing tomorrow?)

✔ **Quer ir para o cinema comigo?** (*keh ee* pah-dah ooh see-*neh*-mah koh-*mee*-goo; Do you want to go to the movies with me?)

Of course, these are all things you say after the very first question: **Qual é seu nome?** (*kwah*-ooh *eh* seh-ooh *noh*-mee; What's your name?) or **Quer dançar?** (*keh* dahn-*sah;* Do you want to dance?)

Chapter 8

When You Gotta Work

. . . .

In This Chapter

▶ Talking on the phone

▶ Making reservations and leaving messages

▶ Discussing professions

▶ Working at the office

. . . .

Dealing with the phone, making appointments, talking about your profession, and sending e-mails are all parts of a day's work. This chapter helps you get through that day in Portuguese.

Picking Up the Phone

In Brazil, most phone numbers have a two-digit prefix for the **cidade** (see-*dah*-jee; city) or a **código regional** (*koh*-jee-goo heh-jee-oh-*nah*-ooh; regional code), which often has a zero in front. The phone number of a famous hotel in Rio called Copacabana Palace, for example, looks like this: (021) 2548-7070. Basic phone numbers have either seven or eight digits. The **código internacional** (*koh*-jee-goh een-teh-nah-see-oh-*nah*-ooh; international calling code) for Brazil is 55.

Here are a few useful phrases Brazilians use when they're dealing with phones:

▮ ✔ **número de telefone** (*noo*-meh-doh jee teh-leh-*foh*-nee; phone number)

▮ ✔ **está errado** (ehs-*tah* eh-*hah*-doh; it's wrong)

- ✔ **está correto** (ehs-*tah* koh-*heh*-toh; it's right)

- ✔ **fazer um telefonema** (fah-*zeh* ooh-m teh-leh-foh-*neh*-mah; to make a phone call)

- ✔ **ligar para alguém** (lee-*gah* pah-dah ah-ooh-*gang*; to call someone)

- ✔ **receber chamadas** (heh-seh-*beh* shah-*mah*-dahz; receive calls)

- ✔ **atender o telefone** (ah-tehn-*deh* ooh teh-leh-*foh*-nee; to answer the phone)

- ✔ **deixar um recado** (day-*shah* oong heh-*kah*-doh; to leave a voicemail message)

- ✔ **telefones celulares** (teh-leh-*foh*-neez sel-loo-*lah*-deez; cell phones)

- ✔ **uma cabina telefônica** (ooh-mah kah-*bee*-nah teh-leh-*foh*-nee-kah; public phone booth) or **orelhão**

You can find plenty of **telefones públicos** (teh-leh-*foh*-nee *poo*-blee-koh; public phones) on Brazilian **ruas.** Locals, always with a sense of humor, call public phones **orelhões** (oh-deh-ooh-*yoh*-eez. *Literally:* big ears) because the phones are housed in a semi-open booth that resembles a three-foot tall **orelha** (oh-*deh*-ooh-yah; ear). All you have to do is **comprar** (kohm-*pdah;* buy) a **cartão telefônico** (kah-*tah*-ooh teh-leh-*foh*-nee-koh; phone card) from any **banca de jornal** (*bahn*-kah jee zhoh-*nah*-ooh; news kiosk) on the **rua** (*hoo*-ah; street).

Saying hello and goodbye

Your phone is ringing. **Não se preocupe** (*nah*-ooh see pdeh-oh-*koo*-pee; Don't sweat it). I'll start with the greeting and goodbye words — they're a cinch.

Perhaps the hotel receptionist is calling you, telling you there's **alguém** (ah-ooh-*gang;* someone) to see you in the lobby. Or **talvez** (*tah*-ooh- *vehz;* maybe) it's your **agente de viagens** (ah-*zhang*-shee jee vee-*ah*-zhangs; travel agent), ready to book your **vôo** (*voh*-ooh; flight) to the Amazon. Either way, answering the call is **fácil** (*fah*-see-ooh; easy).

Here's what you say:

- ✔ **Alô?** (ah-*loh;* Hello? [formal])
- ✔ **Sim?** (sing; Yes?)
- ✔ **Oi.** (*oy*-ee; Hi. [informal])

Here's what you can say before you hang up the phone:

- ✔ **Tchau.** (chow; Bye. *Literally:* Ciao, like in Italian.)
- ✔ **Até logo.** (ah-*teh* loh-goo; Bye. *Literally:* Until soon.)
- ✔ **Até mais.** (ah-*teh* mah-eez; Bye. *Literally:* Until more.)
- ✔ **Até amanhã.** (ah-*teh* ah-mahn-*yah;* Talk to/See you tomorrow. *Literally:* Until tomorrow.)

 Brazilians are very **carinhosos** (kah-deen-yoh-zooz; affectionate). When a **chamada** (shah-*mah*-dah; phone call) ends between two female friends, a male and a female friend, or two family members, Brazilians often say **Um beijo** (oong *bay*-zhoh; A kiss) or **Um abraço** (oong ah-*bdah*-soo; A hug).

Making a call

Making phone calls in a different language can be kind of intimidating, but **você está com sorte!** (voh-*seh* eh-*stah* kohng *soh*-chee; you're in luck!). First, Brazilians typically talk reasonably **devagar** (deh-vah-*gah;* slowly), and they tend to clearly enunciate their syllables. So go native: Relax. **Fique tranqüilo** (*fee*-kee tdahn-*kwee*-loh; Don't worry).

Here are some example sentences about making a call:

- ✔ **Ligo para os Estados Unidos todos os dias.** (*lee*-goh pah-dah ooz eh-*stah*-dooz ooh-*nee*-dohz *toh*-dooz ooz *jee*-ahz; I call the United States every day.)

- ✔ **Ela liga para o namorado dela cinco vezes por dia.** (*eh*-lah *lee*-gah pah-dah ooh nah-moh-*dah*-doh *deh*-lah *seen*-koh *veh*-zeez poh *jee*-ah; She calls her boyfriend five times a day.)

- ✔ **Você liga para a sua mãe muito?** (voh-*seh* lee-gah *pah*-dah ah *soo*-ah *mah*-ee moh-*ee*-toh; Do you call your mom often?)

The verb **ligar** (lee-*gah;* to call) is almost always packaged with **para** — as in **ligar para** (lee-*gah* pah-dah; to call) someone or someplace. To use this expression, use **ligar para** plus the name of the person or place.

Here's a sample conversation of a short phone call:

Operator: **Bom dia. Hotel do Sol Ipanema.** (boh-oong *jee*-ah. oh-*teh*-ooh doo *soh*-ooh eeh-pah-*neh*-mah; Good morning. Sun Hotel, Ipanema.)

Patricia: **Bom dia. Poderia me comunicar com a Roberta Fernandes, quarto número setecentos e oitenta e três, por gentileza?** (boh-oong *jee*-ah. poh-deh-*dee*-ah mee koh-moo-nee-*kah* koh-oong ah hoh-*beh*-tah feh-*nahn*-jeez, *kwah*-toh *noo*-meh-doh seh-chee oh-ee-toh.*tdehz*, poh zhehn-chee-*leh*-zah; Good morning. Could you connect me with Roberta Fernandes, room number 783, please?)

Operator: **Quem fala?** (kang *fah*-lah? Who's calling?)

Patricia: **Sou a Patricia Assunção.** (soh ah pah-*tdee*-see-ah ah-soong-*sah*-ooh; This is Patricia Assunção.)

Operator: **Só um momento, por favor.** (soh oong moh-*mehn*-toh, poh-fah-*voh;* Just a moment, please.)

Words to Know

Poderia me comunicar com . . .	poh-deh-<u>dee</u>-ah mee koh-moo-nee-<u>kah</u> koh-oong	Could you connect me with . . .
por gentileza	poh zhehn-chee- <u>lay</u>-zah	please (formal)
Quem fala?	kang <u>fah</u>-lah	Who's calling?
Sou . . .	soh-ooh	It's . . . (name)
Só um momento.	soh oong moh- <u>mehn</u>-toh	Just a moment.

The expression **ligar para** (to call) someone has a slang meaning. It can also mean "to have a crush on" someone or "to pay attention to" someone or something. **Ele liga muito para ela** (*eh*-lee *lee*-gah moh-*ee*-toh pah-dah *eh*-lah) means "He has a crush on her."

Dealing with verbal mush

The first phone **conversa** (kohn-*veh*-sah; conversation) in any new language is tough. You can't see the person's face as she's talking, or see her body language. You feel **nervoso** (neh-*voh*-zoo; nervous) that you're taking up her valuable time. The connection may be bad. Her **palavras** (pah-*lahv*-dahz; words) come out sounding like mush.

The Brazilian **sotaque** (soh-*tah*-kee; accent) is particularly strange-sounding in the beginning, especially the abundance of nasal vowels throws off even people with a good knowledge of Portuguese words and grammar.

Se não entende (see nah-ooh ehn-*tehn*-jee; If you don't understand) what the person calling you is saying, you can try asking **Fala inglês?** (*fah*-lah eeng-*glehz;* Do you speak English?)

Here's a conversation between coworkers that turns to mush:

Flavia: **Olá, o Carlos está?** (oh-*lah*, ooh *kah*-lohz ehs-*tah?* Hello, is Carlos there?)

Voice on other side: **Krnha estrn galades.** (Unintelligible.)

Flavia: **Poderia falar um pouco mais devagar, por favor?** (poh-deh-*dee*-ah fah-*lah* oong *poh*-koh *mah*-eez deh-vah-*gah*, poh-fah-*voh?* Could you speak a little more slowly, please?)

Voice on other side: **Sod snod manjekof.** (Unintelligible.)

Flavia: **Não estou te escutando. Está ruim a linha.** (*nah*-ooh ehs-*toh* chee ehs-koo-*tahn*-doh. ehs-*tah* hoo-*eeng* ah *leen*-yah. I can't hear you. The connection is bad.)

Voice on other side: **No momento, não se encontra.** (noh moh-*mehn*-toh, *nah*-ooh see ehn-*kohn*-tdah. He's not here right now.)

Flavia: **Ligo mais tarde, obrigada.** (lee-goh mah-eez *tah*-jee, oh-bdee-*gah*-dah. I'll call later, thanks.)

Words to Know

não se encontra	<u>nah-ooh see ehn-</u> <u>kohn</u>-tdah	he/she isn't here (formal)
não está	<u>nah</u>-ooh eh-<u>stah</u>	he/she isn't here (informal)
a linha	ah <u>leen</u>-yah	the phone line

devagar	deh-vah-<u>gah</u>	slowly
mais tarde	<u>mah</u>-eez <u>tah</u>-jee	later
no momento	noh moh-<u>mehn</u>-toh	right now (formal)

If you want to say "right now" and you're not talking on the phone, you can say **agora mesmo** (ah-*goh*-dah *mehs*-moh. *Literally:* right now). **No momento** is frequently used on the phone with strangers because it sounds more formal.

Talking in the past

Sometimes you need to talk about things in the past tense when you're on the phone. Here are some relevant phrases (check out Chapter 2 to see how to conjugate verbs in the past tense):

✔ **Ligaram para você ontem.** (lee-*gah*-dah-ooh pah-dah voh-*seh* ohn-tang; They called you yesterday.)

✔ **Já liguei para ele.** (zhah lee-*gay* pah-dah *eh*-lee; I already called him.) Don't worry that the **eu** (I) form uses the stem **ligu–** while the others use the simple **lig–** stem. This means the verb **ligar** is *irregular* for the **eu** form. But spoken out loud, you can't hear the *u*. So don't sweat it.

✔ **Você não me ligou.** (voh-*seh nah*-ooh mee lee-*goh;* You didn't call me.)

Deixou recado? (day-*shoh* heh-*kah*-doh; Did you leave a message?)

Achamos que ele estava doente. (ah-*shah*-mohz kee *eh*-lee eh-*stah*-vah doh-*ehn*-chee; We thought he was sick.)

✔ **Nós fomos para a praia no domingo.** (nohz *foh*-mooz pah-dah *pdah*-ee-ah noh doh-*ming*-goh; We went to the beach on Sunday.)

✔ **Para onde ela foi?** (pah-dah *ohn*-jee eh-lah *foh-ee*; Where did she go?)

✔ **Eles foram jantar num restaurante.** (eh-leez *foh-*dah-ooh zhahn-*tah* noong heh-stah-ooh-*dahn-*chee; They went to have dinner at a restaurant.)

And check out Table 8-1 for some common time references that signal the past tense.

Table 8-1	Past-Tense Time References	
Term	*Pronunciation*	*Meaning*
ontem	*ohn*-tang	yesterday
na semana passada	nah she-*mah*-mah pah-*sah*-dah	last week
hoje de manhã	*oh*-zhee jee mahn-*yah*	this morning
ontem à noite	*ohn*-tang ah *noh*-ee-chee	last night
faz alguns dias	fah-eez ah-ooh *goonz* jee-ahz	a few days ago
faz vinte minutos	fah-eez *veen*-chee mee- *noo*-tohz	20 minutes ago
faz muito tempo	*fah*-eez moh-*ee*-toh *tehm*-poh	a long time ago
no ano passado	noh *ah*-noh pah-*sah*-doh	last year

Talking about Work

Brazilians generally don't ask you what you do within the first few minutes of meeting you. Some locals consider the question rude. But aside from the Brazilian etiquette about not immediately asking someone about his or her occupation, conversations about work and professions don't vary much from those in other countries. In fact, you may notice that many Portuguese words about work are similar to those in English.

Here are some questions you can ask your new friends when the time's right:

- **Estuda ou trabalha?** (ehs-*too*-dah ooh tdah-*bahl*-yah; Do you study or work?)

- **Qual a sua profissão?** (*kwah*-ooh ah soo-ah pdoh-fee-*sah*-ooh; What's your profession?)

- **Gosta do seu trabalho?** (*goh*-stah doo seh-ooh tdah-*bahl*-yoh; Do you like your work?)

- **Há quanto tempo trabalha nisso?** (ah *kwan*-toh *tang*-poh tdah-*bahl*-yah *nee*-soh; How long have you been in this line of work?)

You can answer these questions in several ways. Some jobs are best expressed by **eu faço . . .** (*eh*-ooh *fah*-soh; I do . . .) plus the name of the profession. For example, **Eu faço . . .**

- **marketing** (*mah*-keh-cheeng; marketing)

- **desenho** (dee-*zehn*-yoh; design)

- **advertising** (*ahj*-veh-*ty*-zeeng; advertising)

- **relações públicas** (heh-lah-*soy*-eez *poob*-lee-kahz; public relations)

- **análise de contas** (ah-*nah*-lah-zee jee *kohn*-tahz; account-analysis)

- **produção de filmes** (pdoh-doo-*sah*-ooh jee *fee*-ooh-meez; film production)

Another common way to express someone's occupation is by saying **trabalha de** plus the name of the job. Someone may ask **Ele/ela faz o quê?** (eh-lee/eh-lah fah-eez ooh *keh;* What does he/she do?). You can respond:

- **Ela trabalha de faxineira.** (*eh*-lah tdah-*bahl*-yah jee fah-shee-*nay*-dah; She works as a cleaning lady.)

- **Ele trabalha de cozinheiro.** (eh-lee tdah-*bahl*-yah jee koh-zing-*yay*-doh; He works as a cook.)

- **Ele trabalha de condutor de ônibus.** (eh-lee tdah-*bahl*-yah jee kohn-doo-*toh* jee *oh*-nee-boos; He works as a bus driver.)

Here are some other ways to respond to questions about profession:

- **Eu trabalho na área de . . .** (*eh*-ooh tdah-*bahl*-yoh nah *ah*-dee-ah jee; I work in the field of . . .)
- **Eu estudo . . .** (*eh*-ooh ehs-*too*-doh; I study . . .)
- **Eu sou . . .** (*eh*-ooh soh; I'm . . . [profession])

Check out Table 8-2 for some common occupations.

Table 8-2	Occupations	
Occupation	*Pronunciation*	*Translation*
estudante	es-too-dahn-chee	student
professor/a	pdoh-feh-*soh*-dah	teacher
médico	*meh*-jee-koh	doctor
advogado/a	ahj-voh-*gah*-doh	lawyer
jornalista	zhoh-nah-*lee*-stah	journalist
banqueiro	bahng-*kay*-doh	banker
cozinheiro	koh-zeen-*yay*-doh	chef
executivo	eh-zeh-koo-*chee*-voh	executive
artista	ah-*chees*-tah	artist
diretor de . . .	jee-deh-*toh* jee	director of . . .
gerente de . . .	jeh-*dang*-chee jee	manager of . . .

The following sample conversation employs profession vocab:

Man: **O que você faz?** (oh *keh* voh-seh *faz*? What do you do?)

Woman: **Sou professora de inglês. E você?** (*soh* pdoh-feh-*soh*-dah jee een-*glehz*. ee voh-seh? I'm an English teacher. And you?)

Man: **Legal. Eu sou advogado.** (lay-*gah*-ooh. *eh*-ooh *soh*-ooh ahj-voh-*gah*-doo; Cool. I'm a lawyer.)

Woman: **Interessante. Você gosta do seu trabalho?** (een-teh-deh-*sahn*-chee. voh-say *goh*-stah doo seh-ooh tdah-*bahl*-yoo? Interesting. Do you like your job?)

Man: **Sim, gosto. E você, há quanto tempo é professora?** (sing, *goh*-stoo. ee voh-*say*, ah *kwahn*-toh *tang*-poh eh pdoh-feh-*soh*-dah? Yeah, I like it. And what about you, how long have you been a teacher?)

Woman: **Faz dez anos que eu sou professora de inglês.** (fah-eez day-eez *ah*-nohz kee *eh*-ooh soh pdoh-feh-*soh*-dah jee een-*glehz*; I've been an English teacher for ten years.)

Words to Know

O que você faz?	oh <u>keh</u> voh-seh <u>faz</u>	What do you do?
há quanto tempo é ... ?	ah <u>kwahn</u>-toh <u>tang</u>- poh eh	How long have you been a ... (profession)?

Faz plus the number of years is a handy way of saying, "It's been (number of years) since ...":

✔ **Faz dez anos que eu não falo inglês.** (fah-eez dehz *ah*-nohz kee *eh*-ooh *nah*-ooh fah-loh eeng-*glehz;* It's been ten years since I've spoken English.)

✔ **Faz um ano que eu estou sem trabalho.** (fah-eez oong *ah*-noh kee *eh*-ooh ehs-*toh* sang tdah-*bahl*-yoh; I've been out of work for a year.)

Or you can say **Faz muito tempo que . . .** to mean "It's been a long time since . . ." without mentioning the number of years. Here's an example:

> **Faz muito tempo que eu fui para o Rio de Janeiro.** (fah-eez moo-*ee*-toh *tang*-poh kee *eh*-ooh *nah*-ooh *voh* pah-dah ooh hee-ooh jee jah-*nay*-doh; It's been a long time since I've been to Rio.)

Dealing with Computers

When you're at the office, here are some typical words that you run in to:

- ✔ **escritório** (eh-skdee-*toh*-dee-oh; office)
- ✔ **caneta** (kah-*neh*-tah; pen)
- ✔ **computador** (kohm-poo-tah-*doh;* computer)
- ✔ **notebook** (notch-*book*-ee; laptop)
- ✔ **responder** (hehs-pohn-*deh;* to answer)
- ✔ **imprimir** (eemp-dee-*mee;* to print out)

When you need to plan a meeting, some of these phrases may come in handy:

Ana: **Bom dia, Carlos. Vamos planejar a reunião?** (boh-oong *jee*-ah *kah*-looz. *vah*-mohz plahn-eh-i ah heh-ooh-nee-*ah*-ooh? Good morning Carlos. Shall we plan the meeting?)

Carlos: **Sim. Vai ser a que horas?** (*sing.* vah-ee seh ah kee *oh*-dahs? Yes. What time will it be?)

Ana: **Às quatorze horas. Convide todo mundo.** (ahz kah-*toh*-zee *oh*-dahz. kohn-*vee*-jee toh-doo *moon*-doh; At two o'clock. Invite everyone.)

Carlos: **OK. Vou enviar um e-mail agora para todos.** (ah-*kay*-ee. voh en-vee-*ah* oong ee-*may*-oh ah-*goh*-dah pah-dah *toh*-dooz; Okay. I'm going to send an e-mail now to everyone.)

Ana: **Perfeito. Depois me manda um e-mail com todos os nomes.** (peh-*fay*-toh. deh-*poy*-eez mee *mahn*-dah oong ee-*may*-oh koh-oong toh-dohz oohz *noh*-meez; Perfect. Afterward, send me an e-mail with all the names.)

Carlos: **Tá bom. Não se preocupe, e eu espero que melhore.** (tah *boh-oong*. *nah*-ooh see pdeh-oh-*koo*-pee poh *ees*-toh, eh *eh*-ooh eh-*sped*-oh kee mehl-*yoh*-dee; Okay. Don't worry, and I hope you get better.)

Words to Know

planejar	plahn-eh-<u>zhah</u>	to plan
reunião	hay-oon-ee-<u>ah</u>-ooh	meeting
enviar	ang-vee-<u>ah</u>	to send
e-mail	ee-<u>may</u>-oh	e-mail
conferência	kohn-feh-<u>dehn</u>-see-ah	conference

Many Brazilians use the Internet. And because they're such social people, they spend a lot of time chatting online. Here are some common words and abbreviations used when e-mailing:

- ✓ **Oi** (Hi)
- ✓ **Olá** (Hello)
- ✓ **Prezado . . .** (Dear . . . [formal])
- ✓ **vc** (you [informal; short for você])
- ✓ **vcs** (you guys [informal; short for vocês])
- ✓ **Abs,** (Hugs, [informal; short for abraços])
- ✓ **Bjs,** (Kisses, [informal; short for beijos])
- ✓ **Saudações,** (Greetings, [formal])
- ✓ **Atenciosamente,** (Attentively, [formal])

The symbol @ in Portuguese is called the **arroba** and is pronounced ah-*hoh*-bah. If you have a period in your e-mail, you may want to remember that's called a **ponto** (*pohn*-toh).

Chapter 9

I Get Around: Transportation

In This Chapter

▶ Choosing transportation

▶ Getting directions

B razil is a vast country, just about the same size as the United States, and the best way to **viajar** (vee-ah-*zhah;* go. *Literally:* to voyage) from place to faraway place is by **ônibus** (*oh*-nee-boos; bus) or **avião** (ah-vee-*ah*-ooh; plane). **Trens** (tdangz; trains) are seldom used. You can also **alugar um carro** (ah-loo-*gah* oong *kah*-hoh; rent a car).

This chapter tells you what you need to get around, from accessing **taxi** services to discussing whether buses are on schedule to asking for directions. Here are a few quick transportation-related phrases:

✔ **Vamos embora!** (*vah*-mooz em-*boh*-dah; Let's go!)

✔ **Como se chega?** (*koh*-moo see *sheh*-gah; How do you get there?)

✔ **Quanto tempo demora para chegar?** (*kwahn*-toh *tehm*-poh deh-*moh*-dah pah-dah sheh-*gah;* How long does it take to get there?)

✔ **Eu vou para . . .** (*eh*-ooh *voh* pah-dah; I'm going to . . .)

- ✔ **Vamos para . . .** (*vah*-mohz pah-dah; We're going to . . .)
- ✔ **Eu fui para . . .** (*eh*-ooh *fwee* pah-dah; I went to . . .)

On the Move: Transportation

Getting where you need to go is very important and knowing the right phrases makes it a whole lot easier. This section gets you moving.

Making a plane reservation

If you're in Brazil for longer than just a few days, you may decide to schedule a **viagem** (vee-*ah*-zhang; trip) somewhere within the country. There are **agências de viagens** (ah-*zhang*-see-ahz jee vee-*ah*-zhangz; travel agencies) all over the place in major cities, so finding one shouldn't be hard. This is where you **fazer uma reserva** (fah-*zeh* ooh-mah heh-*zeh*-vah; make a reservation) for transportation. Here are some questions the agent may ask you:

- ✔ **Olá, posso ajudar?** (oh-*lah* poh-soo ah-zhoo-*dah;* Hello, can I help you?)
- ✔ **Qual é o destino?** (*kwah*-ooh *eh* ooh dehs-*chee*-noo; What is the destination?)
- ✔ **Para quantos dias?** (pah-dah *kwahn*-tooz *jee*-ahz; For how many days?)
- ✔ **Quantos passageiros?** (*kwahn*-tohz pah-sah-*zhay*-dooz; How many passengers?)
- ✔ **Importa o horário do dia?** (eem-*poh*-tah ooh oh-*dah*-dee-ooh doh *jee*-ah; Does the time of day matter?)
- ✔ **Quer reservar o vôo?** (*keh* heh-seh-*vah* ooh *voh;* Do you want to reserve the flight?)
- ✔ **Como vai pagar?** (*koh*-moo *vah*-ee pah-*gah;* How do you want to pay?)

You may want to ask which flight is **mais barato** (*mah-eez bah-dah-toh*; cheaper) or whether the agency can offer you a **pacote** (*pah-koh-chee*; package) that includes the hotel. Here are some other key terms for reserving flights:

- **bilhete** (*beel-yeh-chee*; ticket)
- **assento** (*ah-sehn-too*; seat)
- **janela** (*zhah-neh-lah*; window)
- **corredor** (*koh-heh-doh;* aisle)
- **primeira classe** (*pdee-may-dah klah-see*; first class)
- **classe econômica** (*klah-see eh-koh-noh-mee-kah*; economy class/coach)
- **ida e volta** (*ee-dah ee voh-ooh-tah*; round-trip)
- **somente ida** (*soh-mehn-chee ee-dah*; one-way)
- **de** (*jee*; from)
- **para** (*pah-dah*; to)
- **data da ida** (*dah-tah dah ee-dah*; departure date)
- **data da volta** (*dah-tah dah voh-ooh-tah*; return date)
- **horário dos vôos** (*oh-dah-dee-ooh dooz voh-ooz*; flight schedule)
- **formas de pagamento** (*foh-mahz jee pah-gah-mehn-toh*; method of payment)

The following conversation is one you may have with a travel agent:

Travel agent: **Olá, posso ajudar?** (*oh-lah, poh-soo ah-zhoo-dah;* Hello, can I help you?)

Daniela: **Queria fazer uma reserva para ir para o Rio.** (*kee-dee-ah fah-zeh ooh-mah heh-zeh-vah pah-dah ee pah-dah ooh hee-ooh*; I'd like to make a reservation to go to Rio.)

Travel agent: **Que dia?** (*kee jee-ah*; Which day?)

Daniela: **Na sexta, retornando no domingo.** (nah *sehs*-tah, heh-toh-*nahn*-doh noh doh-*ming*-goh; For Friday, coming back on Sunday.)

Travel agent: **Olha, não sei se tem vaga. Mas vou checar.** (*ohl*-yah, nah-ooh *say* see tang *vah*-gah. mah-eez *voh* sheh-*kah;* To be honest, I don't know if there are any seats. But I'll check.)

Daniela: **Posso retornar também na segunda, de manhãzinha.** (*poh*-soo heh-toh-*nah* tahm-*bang* nah seh-*goon*-dah, jee mahn-yah-*zing*-yah; I can also return on Monday, really early.)

Travel agent: **Aí vai ser mais fácil.** (ah-*ee vah*-ee *seh* mah-eez *fah*-see-ooh; Now that will be easier.)

Daniela: **Fantástico.** (fahn-*tahs*-chee-koh; Fantastic.)

Travel agent: **Tem duas opções — na Gol e na Vasp.** (tang *doo*-ahz ohp-*soh*-eez — nah *goh*-ooh ee nah *vah*-spee; You have two options — on Gol and on Vasp.)

Daniela: **Ótimo.** (*oh*-chee-moh; Great.)

Words to Know

retornando	heh-toh-<u>nahn</u>-doh	returning/coming back
vaga	<u>vah</u>-gah	seat/available spot
checar	sheh-<u>kah</u>	to check
retornar	heh-toh-<u>nah</u>	to return
de manhãzinha	jee mah-yah-<u>zing</u>-yah	really early in the morning
vai ser	<u>vah</u>-ee <u>seh</u> (ok)	it will be
opções	ohp-<u>soh</u>-eez	options

In Brazil, there's usually a **taxa de embarque** (*tah*-shah jee em-*bah*-kee; boarding tax). It's significant for international flights, at around US$80 but only about US$3 for domestic flights. The **taxa** will be included in the quoted flight price.

Here are some useful words and phrases you can use when you travel internationally:

- **comprar um bilhete de avião** (kohm-*pdah* oong beel-*yeh*-chee jee ah-vee-*ah*-ooh; to buy an airline ticket)

- **levar o seu passaporte** (leh-*vah* ooh *seh*-ooh pah-sah-*poh*-chee; to bring your passport)

- **preencher as fichas** (pdehn-*sheh* ahz *fee*-shahz; to fill out forms)

- **a bagagem** (ah bah-*gah*-zhang; the baggage)

- **o visto** (ooh *vee*-stoh; the visa)

- **o consulado** (ooh kohn-soo-*lah*-doh; the consulate)

- **a embaixada** (ah *ehm*-bah-ee-*shah*-dah; the embassy)

- **o aeroporto** (ooh ah-*eh*-doh-*poh*-too; the airport)

- **a alfândega** (ah ah-ooh-*fahn*-deh-gah; Customs)

- **a multa** (ah *mool*-tah; the fine)

- **os impostos** (oohz eem-*poh*-stooz; taxes)

- **a Loja Franca** (ah *loh*-zhah *fdahn*-kah; duty-free)

- **nada a declarar** (*nah*-dah ah deh-klah-*dah;* nothing to declare)

- **a segurança** (ah seh-goo-*dahn*-sah; security)

Check on the Web site of the Brazilian **embaixada** in your **país** (pah-*eez;* country) to find out whether you need a **visto** to enter Brazil.

Taking buses

In Brazil, you can take an **ônibus** (*oh*-nee-boos; bus) to travel long distances between cities or the **ônibus urbano** (*oh*-nee-boos ooh-*bah*-noh; city bus) to get around town. Here are some words to get you started:

- ✔ **passagem de ônibus** (pah-*sah*-zhang jee *oh*-nee-boos; bus ticket)

- ✔ **rodoviária** (hoh-doh-vee-*ah*-dee-ah; central bus station)

- ✔ **poltrona** (pohl-*tdoh*-nah; seat)

- ✔ **origem** (oh-*dee*-zhang; name of city you're traveling from/origin)

- ✔ **destino** (dehs-*chee*-noo; destination)

- ✔ **data** (*dah*-tah; date)

Keep in mind that Brazilians use military time for bus tickets. Eight o'clock at night becomes **às vinte horas** (ahz *veen*-chee *oh*-dahz; at 8 p.m./at 20:00 hours). (See Chapter 3 for more on telling time.)

Check out some phrases you can use either with the **motorista** (moh-toh-*dee*-stah; driver) or another **passageiro** (pah-sah-*zhay*-doo; passenger):

- ✔ **O ônibus está atrasado?** (ooh *oh*-nee-boos eh-*stah* ah-tdah-*zah*-doo; Is the bus late?)

- ✔ **O ônibus sai às onze e quarenta.** (ooh *oh*-nee-boos *sah*-ee ahz *ohn*-zee ee kwah-*den*-tah; The bus leaves at 11:40.)

- ✔ **Vai para . . . ?** (*vah*-ee *pah*-dah; Do you go to . . . ?)

- ✔ **Pára na Rua . . . ?** (*pah*-dah nah *hoo*-ah; Do you stop on . . . Street?)

- ✔ **Quanto é?** (*kwahn*-toh kee *eh*; How much?)

Hailing táxis

Táxis (*talk*-seez; taxis) are plentiful and cheap in Brazil. You can flag one down in the street, just as you would in big cities anywhere else in the world. If you're having trouble finding one, ask someone whether a **ponto de táxi** (*pohn*-toh jee *talk*-see; place where taxis line up to wait for passengers) is nearby.

The **ponto de táxi** consists of a bunch of taxi drivers sitting on a bench, sometimes watching a **novela** (noh-*veh*-lah; soap opera) or **jogo de futebol** (*zhoh*-goo jee foo-chee-*bah*-ooh; soccer match) on an overhead TV.

Here's some taxi talk:

- ✔ **Para . . . por favor.** (pah-dah . . . poh fah-*voh;* To . . . [location], please.)
- ✔ **Sabe como chegar em . . . ?** (*sah*-bee *koh*-moo sheh-*gah* ang; Do you know how to get to . . . ?)
- ✔ **Quanto seria para ir a . . . ?** (*kwahn*-toh seh-*dee*-ah pah-dah ee ah; How much would it be to go to . . . ?)
- ✔ **É perto?** (eh *peh*-too; Is it close?)
- ✔ **É longe?** (eh *lohn*-zhee; Is it far?)

Before you agree to ride, ask the **taxista** (tahk-*sees*-tah; taxi driver) whether he knows where your destination is. Here's a conversation demonstrating taxi talk:

Ricardo: **Olá, é longe o Maracanã?** (oh-*lah*, eh *lohn*-zhee ooh mah-dah-kah-*nah;* Hi. Is Maracanã Stadium far?)

Taxi driver: **Não, e pertinho.** (*nah*-ooh, *eh* peh-*ching*-yoo; No, it's really close.)

Ricardo: **Quanto custaria?** (*kwahn*-toh koos-tah-*dee*-ah; How much would it cost?)

Taxi driver: **Uns dez reais.** (oonz *dez* heh-eyes; About 10 reais.)

Ricardo: **Tá bom.** (tah *boh*-oong; Okay.)

Taxi driver: **É a sua primeira vez no Rio de Janeiro?** (eh ah *soo*-ah pdee-*may*-dah *vez* noh *hee*-ooh jee zhah-*nay*-doh; Is it your first time in Rio?)

Ricardo: **É. E nós estamos muito emocionados ao ver o famoso Maracanã.** (eh. ee nohz eh-*stah*-mooz moh-*ee*-toh eh-moh-see-ooh-*nah*-dooz ah-ooh *veh* ooh fah-*moh*-zoo mah-dah-kah-*nah;* Yeah. And we're really excited to see the famous Maracanã.)

Taxi driver: **Não tem jogo hoje.** (*nah*-ooh *tang* zhoh-goo *oh*-zhee; There's no game today.)

Ricardo: **Tá bom, é só para ver.** (tah *boh*-oong, eh *soh* pah-dah *veh;* That's okay. It's just to take a look.)

Words to Know

pertinho	peh-<u>ching</u>-yoh	very close/close by
uns	oonz	about/some
vez	vez	time
emocionados	eh-<u>moh</u>-see-ooh-<u>nah</u>-dooz	excited
famoso	fah-<u>moh</u>-zoo	famous

Renting a car

If you're the adventurous type, you may decide to **alugar um carro** (ah-loo-*gah* oong *kah*-hoh; rent a car) from a **locadora de carros** (loh-kah-*doh*-dah jee *kah*-hohz; car-rental agency) in Brazil. You're probably already familiar with several international rental agencies in Brazil, like Hertz and Avis. Here are some questions to ask at a **locadora:**

> ✔ **Tem um carro disponível para hoje?** (*tang* oong *kah*-hoh jee-spoh-*nee*-veh-ooh pah-dah *oh*-zhee; Do you have a car available for today?)

✔ **Qual é a tarifa diária para esse modelo?** (*kwah-ooh eh* ah tah-*dee*-fah jee-*ah*-dee-ah pah-dah *eh-see* moh-*deh*-loo; What's the day rate for this [car] make?)

✔ **Tem assistência vinte-quatro horas?** (*tang* ah-see-*stehn*-see-ah *ving*-chee *kwah*-tdoh *oh*-dahz; Do you have 24-hour roadside assistance?)

✔ **Tem alguma promoção?** (*tang* ah-ooh-*goo*-mah pdoh-moh-*sah*-ooh; Do you have any deals/promotions going on?)

✔ **Oferece um plano de seguro?** (oh-feh-*deh*-see oong *plah*-noh jee seh-*goo*-doh; Do you offer an insurance plan?)

You may also want to get familiar with the names of the parts of a car in Portuguese — here are the basics:

✔ **volante** (voh-*lahn*-chee; steering wheel)

✔ **freios** (*fday*-oohz; brakes)

✔ **rodas** (*hoh*-dahz; wheels)

✔ **pára-brisa** (*pah*-dah-*bdee*-sah; windshield)

✔ **motor** (moh-*toh*; engine)

Here are another couple of questions you may need to ask about driving in general:

✔ **As estradas em . . . são boas ou ruins?** (ahz eh-*stdah*-dahz ang . . . *sah*-ooh *boh*-ahz oh hoo-*eenz*; Are the roads in . . . [location] good or bad?)

✔ **Tem um mecânico por aqui?** (*tang* oong meh-*kah*-nee-koh poh ah-*kee*; Is there a mechanic around here?)

The shapes and colors of the **placas** (*plah*-kahz; road signs) in Brazil are pretty much the same as in English-speaking countries.

You may scratch your head when you first visit a **posto de gasolina** (*poh*-stoo jee gah-zoo-*lee*-nah; gas station): In addition to **gasolina,** you sometimes have the option of choosing **álcool** (*ah*-ooh-koh-ooh; alcohol), a fuel made from **cana de açúcar** (*kah*-nah jee ah-*soo*-kah; sugarcane) that's cheaper than **gasolina.** The price difference is about US$2.30 per gallon of alcohol, compared with about US$4 per gallon of gasoline. Many cars made in Brazil use technology that converts the alcohol to car fuel. Ask your rental-shop employees which you can use with your car.

Words to Know

carteira de habilitação	kah-<u>tay</u>-dah jee ah-<u>bee</u>-lee-tah-<u>sah</u>-ooh	driver's license
postos de gasolina	<u>poh</u>-stooz jee gah-zoo-<u>lee</u>-nah	gas stations
tanque de gasolina	<u>tan</u>-kee jee gah-zoh-<u>lee</u>-nah	gas tank
quilometragem livre	<u>kee</u>-loo-meh-<u>tdah</u>-zhang <u>leev</u>-dee	unlimited mileage
retirada	heh-<u>chee</u>-dah-dah	check-out
devolução	deh-voh-loo-<u>sah</u>-ooh	check-in

Onde? Where? The Question for Going Places

The word **onde** (*ohn*-jee; where) can be your best friend as you navigate any new place in Brazil. *Where is . . .* is expressed in three ways: **Onde é** (*ohn*-jee *eh*), **Onde fica** (*ohn*-jee *fee*-kah), and **Onde está** (*ohn*-jee eh-*stah*).

Onde é is used more for people and general locations, whereas **Onde fica** and **Onde está** are used to ask for the precise location of something. **Onde é Macau?** (ohn-jee ee mah-kah-ooh; Where is Macau?) someone asks. They expect to hear an answer like "in Asia," not the precise latitude and longitude of Macau. But by asking **Onde fica aquela loja?** (ohn-jee fee-kah ah-keh-lah loh-zhah; Where is that store?), you expect someone to explain the street, the cross street, and maybe the exact address so that you have no problems finding it. Generally speaking, **onde fica** is more commonly used than **onde está**.

Check out some common variations of phrases that use **onde**:

- **Para onde . . . ?** (pah-dah ohn-jee; To where . . . ?)
- **Onde é . . . ?** (ohn-jee eh; Where is . . . ?)
- **Sabe onde fica . . . ?** (sah-bee ohn-jee fee-kah; Do you know where . . . is located?)
- **Sabe onde tem . . . ?** (sah-bee ohn-jee tang; Do you know where there's a . . . ?)
- **De onde . . . ?** (jee ohn-jee; From where . . . ?)

Here are some sentences that use **onde** phrases:

- **Para onde vai esse ônibus?** (pah-dah ohn-jee vah-ee eh-see oh-nee-boos; Where does this bus go to?)
- **Onde é a Rua Pedralbes?** (ohn-jee eh ah hoo-ah peh-drah-ooh-beez; Where is Pedralbes Street?)
- **Sabe onde fica o Citibank?** (sah-bee ohn-jee fee-kah ooh see-chee-bahn-kee; Do you know where the Citibank is located?)
- **Sabe onde tem um supermercado?** (sah-bee ohn-jee tang oong soo-peh-meh-kah-doh; Do you know where there's a supermarket?)
- **De onde é o cantor?** (jee ohn-jee eh ooh kahn-toh; Where is the singer from?)

Another useful phrase is **Estou procurando . . .** (eh-*stoh* pdoh-koo-*dahn*-doh; I'm looking for . . .). The phrase uses the verb **procurar** (*pdoh*-koo-*dah;* to look/search for). The verb is related to the old-fashioned word *procure* in English.

Here's a conversation using various *where* phrases:

Silvio: **Por favor, sabe onde passa o ônibus número sessenta e dois?** (poh fah-*voh, sah*-bee *ohn*-jee *pah*-sah ooh *oh*-nee-boos *noo*-meh-doh seh-*sehn*-tah ee *doh*-eez; Excuse me, do you know where bus number 62 passes?)

Passerby: **Para onde quer ir?** (pah-dah *ohn*-jee *keh ee;* Where would you like to go?)

Silvio: **Quero ir para Petrópolis.** (*keh*-doo ee pah-dah peh-*tdoh*-poh-leez; I want to go to Petropolis.)

Passerby: **Não conheço o sessenta e dois, mas o quarenta e três vai para Petrópolis.** (*nah*-ooh kohn-*yeh*-soo ooh seh-*sehn*-tah ee *doh*-eez, *mah*-eez ooh kwah-*dehn*-tah ee *tdehz vah*-ee pah-dah ooh peh-*tdoh*-poh-leez; I don't know the number 62, but the 43 goes to Petropolis.)

Silvio: **Sabe onde tem uma parada do quarenta e três?** (*sah*-bee *ohn*-jee *tang* ooh-mah pah-*dah*-dah doo kwah-*dehn*-tah ee *tdehz?;* Do you know where there's a bus stop for the 43?)

Passerby: **Tem uma do lado do Pão de Açúcar. Sabe onde é?** (*tang ooh*-mah doo *lah*-doo doo *pah*-ooh jee ah-*soo*-kah. *sah*-bee *ohn*-jee *eh;* There's one next to the Pão de Açúcar. Do you know where it is?)

Silvio: **Não, não sei.** (*nah*-ooh, *nah*-ooh *say;* No, I don't.)

Passerby: **Fica naquela esquina. Tá vendo?** (*fee*-kah nah-*keh*-lah eh-*skee*-nah. tah *vehn*-doh?; It's on that corner. Do you see it?)

Words to Know

passa	pah-sah	passes
ônibus	oh-nee-boos	bus
número	noo-meh-doh	number
conheço	kohn-yeh-soh	I know/I'm familiar with
vai	vah-ee	goes
parada	pah-dah-dah	bus stop
do lado	doo lah-doo	next to
naquela	nah-keh-lah	on that
esquina	eh-skee-nah	street corner
Tá vendo?	tah vehn-doh	Do you see it?

Understanding Spatial Directions

You can use the descriptions of space in Table 9-1 while asking for directions in a city, trying to **encontrar** (ehn-kohn-tdah; find) something in someone's **casa** (kah-zah; house), or even while taking an **axé** (ah-sheh; Brazilian-style aerobics) class.

Table 9-1	Words That Describe Locations	
Term	*Pronunciation*	*Translation*
na frente	nah *fdehn*-chee	in front of
atrás	ah-*tdah*-eez	behind

(continued)

Table 9-1 *(continued)*

Term	Pronunciation	Translation
para a direita	*pah*-dah ah jee-day-tah	to the right
para a esquerda	*pah*-dah ah ehs-*keh*-dah	to the left
abaixo	ah-*bah*-ee-shoh	below/underneath
acima	ah-*see*-mah	above/on top of
do lado	doo *lah*-doh	next to
dentro	*dehn*-tdoh	inside
for a	*foh*-dah	outside

Here are some sentences that use directional words and phrases:

- ✔ **Fica na frente do Correio.** (*fee*-kah nah *fdehn*-chee doo koh-*hay*-oh; It's in front of the post office.)

- ✔ **Está atrás da mesa.** (eh-*stah* ah-*tdah*-eez dah *meh*-zah; It's behind the table.)

- ✔ **Vá para a direita.** (*vah* pah-dah ah jee-*day*-tah; Go to the right.)

- ✔ **Fica para a esquerda da loja.** (*fee*-kah *pah*-dah ah ehs-*keh*-dah dah *loh*-zhah; It's to the left of the store.)

- ✔ **Olhe embaixo.** (*ohl*-yee em-*bah*-ee-shoh; Look underneath.)

- ✔ **Estão em cima da geladeira.** (eh-*stah*-ooh ah-*see*-mah dah zheh-lah-*day*-dah; They're on top of the refrigerator.)

- ✔ **Está do lado da janela.** (eh-*stah* doo *lah*-doh dah zhah-*neh*-lah; It's next to the window.)

✔ **Está dentro da caixa.** (eh-*stah dehnt*-droh dah *kah*-ee-shah; It's inside the box.)

✔ **O carro está fora da garagem.** (ooh *kah*-hoh eh-*stah foh*-dah dah gah-*dah*-zhang; The car's outside of the garage.)

Straight ahead can be expressed a couple of ways: **direto** (jee-*deh*-too. *Literally:* direct) or **reto** (*heh*-too. *Literally:* straight). If you're driving, someone may tell you

✔ **Pode ir reto.** (*poh*-jee *ee heh*-too; You can go straight.)

✔ **Segue sempre direto.** (*seh*-gee *sehm*-pdee jee-*deh*-too; It's straight ahead, all the way. *Literally:* It's all straight.)

Navigating Cityscapes

Some Brazilian cities can be a challenge to figure out, but the following terms will help you get your bearings:

✔ **museu** (moo-*zeh*-ooh; museum)

✔ **galeria de arte** (gah-leh-*dee*-ah jee *ah*-chee; art gallery)

✔ **centro da cidade** (*sent*-droh dah see-*dah*-jee; city center)

✔ **bairro** (*bah*-ee-hoo; neighborhood)

✔ **centro histórico** (*sehn*-tdoh ee-*stoh*-dee-koh; historic center)

✔ **quarteirão** (kwah-tay-*dah*-oong; block)

✔ **praça** (*pdah*-sah; plaza)

✔ **rua** (*hoo*-ah; street)

✔ **rio** (*hee*-ooh; river)

✔ **parque** (*pah*-kee; park)

- ✔ **centro comercial** (*sehn*-tdoh koh-meh-see-*ah*-ooh; shopping center)
- ✔ **jardim** (zhah-*jing;* garden)
- ✔ **mar** (mah; ocean)
- ✔ **beira-mar** (bay-dah-*mah;* shoreline/seafront)
- ✔ **morro** (*moh*-hoo; hill)
- ✔ **igreja** (ee-*gdeh*-zhah; church)
- ✔ **ponte** (*pohn*-chee; bridge)

Here are some words you can use to give directions:

- ✔ **vá** (vah; go)
- ✔ **cruza** (*kdoo*-zah; cross)
- ✔ **olha** (*ohl*-yah; look)
- ✔ **pega** (*peh*-gah; take)
- ✔ **segue** (*seh*-gee; follow)
- ✔ **sobe** (*soh*-bee; go up)
- ✔ **desce** (*deh*-see; go down)

To give directions, use the *command* or *imperative* verb form. In Portuguese, you can give commands to someone by using the **você** form of the verb. Simply use the *a* ending for **–ar** verbs or the *e* ending for **–er/–ir** verbs. The verb **ir** (ee; to go), however, is irregular; it takes the form **vá** (vah) for commands. Just like in English, the subject of the sentence (you/**você**) is implied, so you can start the sentence with the verb: **Cruza a ponte** (*kdoo*-zah ah *pohn*-chee; Cross the bridge).

Getting directions straight is hard enough in English — let alone in Portuguese! So here are sample sentences that put together some of the terms that have to do with location:

✔ **Está atrás da igreja.** (eh-*stah* ah-*tdah*-eez dah ee-*gdeh*-zhah; It's behind the church.)

✔ **Fica na beira-mar.** (*fee*-kah nah *bay*-dah *mah;* It's on the seafront.)

✔ **Olha para lá.** (*ohl*-yah *pah*-dah *lah;* Look over there.)

✔ **Pega a segunda à direita.** (*peh*-gah ah seh-*goon*-dah ah jee-*day*-tah; Take the second right.)

✔ **Segue essa rua direto.** (*seh*-gee *eh*-sah *hoo*-ah jee-*deh*-toh; Follow this road all the way.)

You may want to use some of these handy connector words, which help tell you when to do something:

✔ **quando** (*kwahn*-doh; when)

✔ **antes** (*ahn*-cheez; before)

✔ **depois** (deh-*poh*-eez; after)

✔ **logo** (*loh*-goo; as soon as)

✔ **até** (ah-*teh;* until)

Just for fun, here are some more-complicated sentences that show you how you can use those connector words:

✔ **Vá até a praça, e depois pega a Rua Almirantes.** (*vah* ah-*teh* ah *pdah*-sah ee deh-*poh*-eez *peh*-gah ah *hoo*-ah ah-ooh-mee-*dahn*-cheez; Go until you reach the plaza, and then take Almirantes Street.)

✔ **Sobe a Faria Lima, e depois pega a Bandeirantes quando chegar no posto de gasolina.** (*soh*-bee ah fah-*dee*-ah *lee*-mah ee deh-*poh*-eez *peh*-gah ooh bahn-day-*dahn*-cheez *kwahn*-doh sheh-*gah* noo *poh*-stoo jee *gah*-zoh-*lee*-nah; Go up Faria Lima, and then take Bandeirantes when you get to the gas station.)

Over Here, Over There

Take a look at how you can say *here, there,* and *over there.* You can use these words in so many settings — when you're asking for directions, browsing in a shop, or pointing out a person on the street. These terms help you distinguish the physical position of the item or person in relation to your location.

- **aqui** (ah-*kee;* here)
- **ali** (ah-*lee;* there)
- **lá** (lah; over there)

In general, **lá** is reserved for places that are a few minutes' walk away or more. If you're talking about an object upstairs, use **ali.** If you're talking about your car parked on the other side of town, use **lá.** Also use **lá** to talk about stuff happening really far away, like in other countries. Here are some examples:

- **Estamos aqui.** (eh-*stah*-mohz ah-*kee;* We're here.)
- **Está ali, na mesa.** (eh-*stah* ah-*lee* nah *meh*-zah; It's there, on the table.)
- **Lá nos Estados Unidos, se come muita fast food.** (*lah* nohz eh-*stah*-dohz ooh-*nee*-dooz, see *koh*-mee moh-*ee*-tah fast food; Over there in the United States, they eat a lot of fast food.) (*Note:* Brazilians say *fast food* in English.)
- **Vá lá.** (*vah* lah; Go over there.)

Say you're in a taxi. You've told the driver the street where you're going, but now you're on that street and want to say, "Let me off right here." Say **aqui-o!** (ah-*kee-ah;* Right here!) to sound like a native Brazilian.

The one time you won't use **aqui** when you mean *here* is with the expression *Come here,* where **cá** replaces **aqui: Vem cá!** (vang *kah;* Come here!), a mother says to her child.

How Far? Perto ou longe?

One question you may want to ask before hearing a complicated set of directions is **Fica longe?** (*fee*-kah *lohn*-zhee; Is it far?). Here are some handy words you can use for estimating distances:

- ✔ **longe** (*lohn*-zhee; far)
- ✔ **perto** (*peh*-too; close)
- ✔ **muito longe** (moh-*ee*-toh *lohn*-zhee; really far)
- ✔ **muito perto** (moh-*ee*-toh *peh*-too; really close)
- ✔ **pertinho** (peh-*cheen*-yoh; really close)

Practice near and far with the following conversation:

Taís: **Por favor, qual fica mais perto, o shopping ou a praia?** (poh fah-*voh*, *kwah*-ooh *fee*-kah *mah*-eez *peh*-too, ooh *shoh*-ping ooh ah *pdah*-ee-ah; Excuse me, which is closer, the shopping mall or the beach?)

Concierge: **A praia é bem mais perto. Fica aqui do lado.** (ah *pdah*-ee-ah eh *bang* mah-eez *peh*-too. *fee*-kah ah-*kee* doo *lah*-doo; The beach is much closer. It's just on the other side of here.)

Taís: **E o shopping? Como se chega?** (ee ooh *shoh*-ping? *koh*-moh see *sheh*-gah?; And the mall? How do you get there?)

Concierge: **Olha, tem que pegar dois ônibus, ou pode ir de táxi.** (*ohl*-yah, *tang* kee peh-*gah* doh-eez *oh*-nee-boos, oh *poh*-jee *eeh* jee *tahk*-see; Well, you have to take two buses, or you can take a taxi.)

Taís: **Tudo bem. O shopping para ir hoje parece longe demais.** (too-doh *bang*. ooh *shoh*-ping pah-dah *eeh* oh-zhee pah-*deh*-see *lohn*-zhee jee-*mah*-eez; All right. The mall seems too far away to go to today.)

Concierge: **Melhor ficar tranqüila na praia.** (mel-*yoh* fee-*kah* tdahn-*kwee*-lah nah *pdah*-ee-ah; It's better to relax on the beach.)

Words to Know

mais perto	mah-eez peh-too	closer
bem mais perto	bang mah-eez peh-too	a lot closer
tem que pegar . . .	tang kee peh-gah	you have to take . . .
pode	poh-jee	you can
ir de táxi	eeh jee tahk-see	go by taxi
parece	pah-deh-see	it seems
longe demais	lohn-zhee jee mah-eez	too far
ficar tranqüila	fee-kah tdahn-kwee-lah	to relax

Chapter 10

Finding a Place to Lay Your Weary Head

. . . .

In This Chapter
▶ Finding a home
▶ Scoping out a hotel
▶ Talking about sleep

. . . .

*W*hether you've been working at the office or out shopping and seeing the sights, you need a place to lay your head. This chapter gives you the phrases you need to find a house or a hotel.

Finding a Place to Live

Most Brazilians in cities live in apartments, and most Brazilians in rural areas live in houses — like most people in the world. If you're staying in Brazil for a while and need to rent a place to stay, you may find that renting an apartment in Brazil is a little different from renting an apartment in the United States.

Here are some questions you may want to ask the landlord of an apartment you're interested in:

▶ **Fica em qual andar?** (*fee*-kah ang kwah-ooh ahn-*dah;* What floor is it on?)

▶ **Que tipo de vista tem?** (kee chee-poh jee *vee*-stah tang; What type of a view does it have?)

✔ **Quanto é o aluguel?** (*kwahn*-toh eh ooh ah-loo-*geh*-ooh; How much is the rent?)

✔ **Tem ar condicionado?** (tang *ah* kohn-dee-see-ooh-*nah*-doo; Does it have air-conditioning?)

✔ **Quantos metros quadrados?** (*kwahn*-tohs *meht*-dohs kwah-*drah*-dohs; How many square meters?)

✔ **Vem incluída a luz?** (vang een-kloo-*ee*-dah ah *looz;* Is electricity included?)

✔ **Tem estacionamento?** (tang eh-stah-see-oh-nah-*mehn*-toh; Does it have a parking spot?)

Take a look at Table 10-1 for some basic words that you may want to use when you discuss accommodations or start to furnish your apartment:

Table 10-1	Living-Space Words	
Term	**Pronunciation**	**Translation**
casa	*kah*-zah	house
apartamento	ah-*pah*-tah-*mehn*-toh	apartment
porta	*poh*-tah	door
quarto	*kwah*-toh	room
banheiro	bahn-*yay*-doh	bathroom
terraço	teh-*hah*-soh	balcony
jardim	zhah-*jing*	garden
piscina	pee-*see*-nah	pool
cozinha	koh-*zing*-yah	kitchen
luz	looz	light
janela	zhah-*neh*-lah	window
geladeira	zheh-lah-*day*-dah	refrigerator
fogão	foh-*gah*-ooh	stove

Term	Pronunciation	Translation
mesa	*meh*-zah	table
cadeira	kah-*day*-dah	chair
sofá	soh-*fah*	sofa
cama	*koo*-mah	bed
travesseiro	tdah-veh-*say*-dah	pillow
lençóis	lehn-*soh*-eez	sheets
escrivaninha	ehs-kdee-vah-*nee*-ah	desk
televisão	teh-leh-vee-*zah*-ooh	television

Brazilians call the first floor of a building the **térreo** (*teh*-hee-oh; ground), and what people call in English the second floor, they call the **primeiro andar** (pdee-*may-doh* ahn-*dah;* first floor). A tad confusing at first, but fairly easy to get used to!

Checking Out the Hotel or Pousada

In Brazil, there are two main types of **hospedagem** (oh-speh-*dah*-zhang; lodging). **Hotéis** (oh-*tay*-eez; hotels) are very large and and may have lots of amenities, and **pousadas** (poh-*zah*-dahz; guesthouses) are small and friendly.

Deciding where to stay

Before you decide where to stay, you want to **revisar** (heh-vee-*zah;* check out) the **quartos** (*kwah*-tooz; rooms) and the place in general, **dentro** (*dehn*-tdoh; inside) and **fora** (*foh*-dah; outside). You'll want to ask some **perguntas** (peh-*goon*-tahz; questions), too.

Hotels are a great place to use the expression
Tem . . . ? (tang; Does it have/Do you have . . . ?).
Here are some **perguntas** you can use to ask about
o quarto:

- ✔ **Tem água quente?** (*tang* ah-gwah *kang*-chee;
  Does it have hot water?)

- ✔ **Tem banheira?** (*tang* bahn-*yay*-dah; Does it have
  a bathtub?)

- ✔ **Tem ar condicionado?** (tang *ah* kohn-*dee*-see-
  ooh-*nah*-doo; Does it have air-conditioning?)

- ✔ **Tem ventilador?** (tang vehn-chee-lah-*doh;* Does
  it have a fan?)

- ✔ **Tem cofre?** (tang *koh*-fdee; Does it have a safe
  deposit box?)

- ✔ **Tem vista?** (tang *vee*-stah; Does it have a view?)

- ✔ **Tem acesso à Internet?** (tang ahk-*seh*-soo *ah*
  een-teh-*neh*-chee; Does it have Internet access?)

- ✔ **Tem TV a cabo?** (tang teh-*veh* ah *kah*-boh; Does
  it have cable TV?)

- ✔ **Tem Jacuzzi?** (*tang* zhah-*koo*-zee; Does it have a
  Jacuzzi?)

And here's what you can ask about the **hotel** (oh-*tay*-
ooh; hotel) or **pousada** (poh-*zah*-dah; guesthouse) in
general:

- ✔ **Tem café incluído?** (*vang* een-kloo-*ee*-doh ooh
  kah-*feh;* Is breakfast included?)

- ✔ **Tem piscina?** (tang pee-*see*-nah; Do you have a
  pool?)

- ✔ **Tem quarto para não fumantes?** (tang *kwah*-toh
  pah-dah *nah*-ooh foo-*mahn*-cheez; Do you have
  nonsmoking rooms?)

- ✔ **Tem academia?** (tang ah-kah-deh-*mee*-ah; Do
  you have a gym?)

This phrase doesn't use **tem,** but you can use it to ask
about one of the hotel services: **Oferecem transporte**

do aeroporto? (oh-feh-*deh*-sehn tdahn-*spoh*-chee doo ah-eh-doh-*poh*-too; Do you offer a pickup service from the airport?).

Making reservations

You can use the preceding questions and phrases about **hospedagem** (oh-speh-*dah*-zhang; accommodations) either on the phone, when you're making a **reserva** (heh-*seh*-vah; reservation), or in person, at the **recepção do hotel** (heh-sep-*sah*-ooh doo oh-*teh*-ooh; hotel reception desk). (For more on talking on the phone, see Chapter 8.)

If you can do so, trying to **fazer uma reserva** (fah-*zeh* ooh-mah heh-*seh*-vah; make a reservation) before you **chegar** (sheh-*gah;* arrive) is always a good idea. The most important question, of course, is whether the place has a **vaga** (*vah*-gah; vacancy). Here are some helpful phrases:

- ✔ **Tem vaga para hoje à noite?** (tang *vah*-gah pah-dah *oh*-zhee ah *noh*-ee-chee; Do you have a vacancy for tonight?)

- ✔ **Tem vaga para o fim de semana?** (*tang vah*-gah pah-dah ooh *fing* jee seh-*mah*-nah; Do you have a vacancy for the weekend?)

- ✔ **Tem vaga para o mês que vem?** (tang *vah*-gah pah-dah ooh *mehz* kee *vang;* Do you have a vacancy for next month?)

- ✔ **Eu quero fazer uma reserva.** (*eh*-ooh kee-*dee*-ah fah-*zeh* ooh-mah heh-*seh*-vah; I want to make a reservation.)

- ✔ **É para duas pessoas.** (*eh* pah-dah *doo*-ahz peh-*soh*-ahz; It's for two people.)

- ✔ **Só para uma pessoa.** (*soh* pah-dah *ooh*-mah peh-*soh*-ah; Just for one person.)

The hotel clerk may ask or tell you:

- ✔ **Quantas pessoas?** (*kwahn*-tahz peh-*soh*-ahz; How many people?)

✔ **Por quantas noites?** (poh *kwahn*-tahz *noh*-ee-cheez; For how many nights?)

✔ **Cama de casal, ou duas camas de solteiro?** (*kah*-mah jee kah-*zah*-ooh, ooh *doo*-ahz *kah*-mahz jee soh-ooh-*tay*-doh; A double bed, or two twin beds?)

Checking in and checking out: Registration procedures

Funnily enough, most Brazilians refer to *the check-in process* as **o check-in** (ooh sheh-*king*). **Fazer o check-in** (fah-*zeh* ooh sheh-*king*) means "to check in."

Checking into a **hotel** (oh-*tay*-ooh; hotel) or **pousada** (poh-*zah*-dah; guesthouse) in Brazil is the same process as you'd see in most places around the world. First, you give the desk clerk your **nome** (*noh*-mee; name). If you have a **reserva** (heh-*seh*-vah; reservation), the clerk will probably check the **detalhes** (deh-*tah*-leez; details) on file for you and then give you the **chaves** (*shah*-veez; keys) to the room. On the way to your **quarto** (*kwah*-too; room), a hotel worker will probably point out important places in the **prédio** (*pdehj*-ee-yoo; building), like where you'll be eating **café da manhã** (kah-*feh* dah mahn-*yah;* breakfast) and where the **academia** (ah-kah-deh-*mee*-ah; gym) and **piscina** (pee-*see*-nah; pool) are, if it's a large hotel.

By federal law, every **hotel** and **pousada** has to give every **hóspede** (*oh*-speh-jee; guest) a **ficha** (*fee*-shah; form) to fill out, which asks you to write down basic I.D. information, as well as which places you've visited in Brazil so far and which places you're headed to. This **ficha** helps **Embratur** (em-bdah-*too;* the federal tourism board) understand the activity of its tourists. The **ficha** uses the following terms:

✔ **nome** (*noh*-mee; first name)

✔ **sobrenome** (*soh*-bdee *noh*-mee; last name/surname)

✔ **país de origem** (pah-*eez* jee oh-*dee*-zhang; country of origin)

✔ **data** (*dah*-tah; date)

✔ **próximo destino** (*pdoh*-see-moh dehs-*chee*-noo; next destination)

✔ **número de passaporte** (*noo*-meh-doh jee pah-sah-*poh*-chee; passport number)

The following are some phrases that the hotel clerk may use:

✔ **Aqui tem duas chaves.** (ah-*kee* tang *doo*-ahz *shah*-veez; Here are two keys.)

✔ **Preencha essa ficha, por favor.** (*pdehn*-sha *eh*-sah *fee*-shah poh fah-*voh*; Fill out this form, please.)

Talking about Sleep

Whether you're going home after a long day at work or after sightseeing 'til you're ready to drop, the following phrases show you how to say how tired you are or to talk about sleep in general:

✔ **Dormiu bem?** (doh-*mee*-ooh *bang*; Did you sleep well?)

✔ **Dormi muito mal.** (doh-*mee* moh-*ee*-toh *mah*-ooh; I slept really poorly.)

✔ **Dormi como uma pedra.** (doh-*mee* koh-moo *ooh*-mah *ped*-rah; I slept like a rock — Brazilian for *I slept like a log.*)

✔ **Dormimos só quatro horas.** (doo-*mee*-mooz *soh* *kwah*-tdoh *oh*-dahz; We slept only four hours.)

✔ **Eu preciso dormir oito horas.** (*eh*-ooh pdeh-*see*-zoo doo-*mee* *oh*-ee-toh *oh*-dahz; I need to sleep eight hours.)

✔ **Os gatos dormem no meu quarto.** (ooz *gah*-tohz *doo*-mang noh *meh*-ooh *kwah*-too; The cats sleep in my room.)

✔ **Adoro dormir na praia.** (ah-*doh*-doo doh-*mee* nah *pdah*-ee-ah; I love sleeping on the beach.)

✔ **Vou dormir. Boa noite.** (*voh* doo-*mee. boh*-ah *noh*-ee-chee; I'm going to bed. Good night.)

✔ **Você deveria ir dormir cedo hoje.** (voh-*seh* deh-veh-*dee*-ah *ee* doo-*mee* seh-doo *oh*-zhee; You should go to sleep early today.)

✔ **Não funciono se durmo menos de cinco horas.** (*nah*-ooh foon-see-*oh*-noo see *doo*-moh *meh*-nohz jee *seen*-koh *oh*-dahz; I can't function if I sleep less than five hours.)

A useful sleep-related phrase is **estar com sono** (eh-*stah* kohng *soh*-noo; to be sleepy):

✔ **Está com sono?** (eh-*stah* kohng *soh*-noo; Are you sleepy?)

✔ **Estou com sono.** (eh-*stoh* kohng *soh*-noo; I'm sleepy.)

Hopefully, you'll never have **pesadelos** (*peh*-zah-*deh*-looz; nightmares) — only **sonhos doces** (*sohn*-yooz *doh*-seez; sweet dreams)!

Acorda! (ah-*koh*-dah; Wake up!) is what a Brazilian may say if you haven't set your **despertador** (deh-*speh*-tah-*doh;* alarm clock) properly. Here are some other phrases related to waking up:

✔ **Acordei cedo.** (ah-koh-*day seh*-doh; I woke up early.)

✔ **Acordei tarde.** (ah-koh-*day tah*-jee; I woke up late.)

✔ **Poderia me acordar às oito horas?** (poh-deh-*dee*-ah mee ah-koh-*dah* ahz *oh*-ee-toh *oh*-dahz; Could you wake me up at 8 o'clock?)

✔ **A que horas tem que acordar amanhã?** (ah *kee oh*-dahz *tang* kee ah-koh-*dah* ah-mahn-*yah?;* What time do you have to wake up tomorrow?)

Words to Know

A que horas . . . ?	ah kee oh-dahz	At what time . . . ?
tem que acordar	<u>tang</u> kee ah-koh-<u>dah</u>	you have to wake up
. . . hein?	ang	. . . right?
você deveria	voh-<u>seh</u> <u>deh</u>-veh-<u>dee</u>-ah	you should
ir dormir	<u>eeh</u> doh-<u>mee</u>	to go to sleep
cedo	<u>seh</u>-doo	early
menos de	<u>meh</u>-nohz <u>jee</u>	less than

Chapter 11

Dealing with Emergencies

....

In This Chapter

▶ Shouting for help after a robbery or other incident

▶ Preventing illness and getting medical help

▶ Talking about legal problems

....

*E*mergencies can happen anywhere, and you can handle them best if you're prepared. This chapter tells you how to deal with life's unexpected adventures.

Here are some basic emergency terms to start you out:

- ✔ **Cuidado!** (kwee-*dah*-doh; Watch out!)
- ✔ **Rápido!** (*hah*-pee-doh; Quick!)
- ✔ **Vamos!** (*vah*-mooz; Let's go!)
- ✔ **Me ajuda!** (mee ah-*zhoo*-dah; Help me!)
- ✔ **Fogo!** (*foh*-goo; Fire!)

Stick 'em Up: What to Say If You're Robbed

So what should you do if you're being robbed? The local refrain is **Não reaja** (*nah*-ooh hee-*ah*-zhah; Don't react). That means: Don't shout, don't try to get away, don't punch the **ladrão** (lah-*drah*-ooh; robber/ pickpocket).

Saying nothing during a robbery is generally best, but here are some classic phrases you may want to know:

- ✔ **Não tenho dinheiro.** (*nah*-ooh *tang*-yoh jing-*yay*-doh; I don't have any money.)

- ✔ **Não tenho nada.** (*nah*-ooh *tang*-yoh *nah*-dah; I don't have anything.)

- ✔ **Socorro!** (soh-*koh*-hoo; Help!)

- ✔ **É ladrão!** (*eh* lah-*drah*-ooh; He's a robber/pick-pocket!)

Of course, you want to try to avoid having any problems in Brazil. Besides taking the same safety precautions you'd take back at home, it's always a good idea to ask locals whether a certain area is safe:

- ✔ **Esta região é segura?** (*eh*-stah heh-zhee-*ah*-ooh eh seh-*goo*-dah; Is this area safe?)

- ✔ **Quais os bairros que são perigosos?** (*kwah*-eez oohz *bah*-ee-hooz kee *sah*-ooh peh-dee-*goh*-zooz; Which neighborhoods are dangerous?)

Asking for and receiving help

Say you've just been robbed. You had only a little money on you, and the robber didn't get anything else. You now need to get back home or to your hotel.

For this situation, or any other time you need help for something that's not a major emergency, you can use these phrases:

✔ **Por favor, poderia me ajudar?** (poh fah-*voh* poh-deh-*dee*-ah mee ah-zhoo-*dah;* Excuse me, could you help me?)

✔ **Eu preciso de ajuda, por favor.** (*eh*-ooh pdeh-*see*-zoo jee ah-*zhoo*-dah, poh fah-*voh;* I need help, please.)

✔ **Por favor, posso usar o seu telefone?** (poh fah-*voh*, poh-soh ooh-*zah* ooh seh-ooh teh-leh-*foh*-nee?; Excuse me, could I use your phone?)

✔ **Preciso ligar para o consulado.** (pdeh-*see*-zoo lee-*gah* pah-dah ooh kohn-soo-*lah*-doo; I need to call the consulate.)

✔ **Tem o número da polícia local?** (*tang* ooh noo-meh-doh dah poh-*lee*-see-ah loh-*kah*-ooh?; Do you have the number for the local police?)

Conversely, what can you say if Brazilians offer you **ajuda** (ah-*zhoo*-dah; help)? Try these responses:

✔ **Obrigado/a, sim, eu preciso de ajuda.** (oh-bdee-*gah*-doh/dah sing *eh*-ooh pdeh-*see*-zoo jee ah-*zhoo*-dah; Thanks, yes, I need help.)

✔ **Estou bem, obrigado/a.** (*eh*-*stoh bang,* oh-bdee-*gah*-doh/dah; I'm fine, thanks.)

✔ **Não preciso de ajuda.** (*nah*-ooh pdeh-*see*-zoo jee ah-*zhoo*-dah; I don't need any help.)

✔ **Eu prefiro ficar sozinho/a.** (*eh*-ooh pdeh-*fee*-doo fee-*kah* soh-*zeen*-yoh/yah; I prefer to be alone.)

Words to Know

seqüestros	seh-<u>kweh</u>-stdros	lightning-
relâmpagos	heh-<u>lahm</u>-pah-gohz	speed
		kidnappings

continued

Words to Know (continued)

ladrão	lah-<u>drah</u>-ooh	robber/ pickpocket
carteira	kah-<u>tay</u>-dah	wallet
relógio	heh-<u>loh</u>-zhee-ooh	watch
bolsa	<u>boh</u>-ooh-sah	purse
ligar para	lee-<u>gah</u> pah-dah	to call
consulado	kohn-soo-<u>lah</u>-doh	consulate
número	<u>noo</u>-meh-doh	phone number
polícia local	poh-<u>lee</u>-see-ah loh <u>kah</u>-ooh	local police
delegacia	deh-leh-gah-<u>see</u>-ah	police station

Reporting a problem to the police

Most Brazilians will tell you they fear **a polícia** (ah poh-*lee*-see-ah; the police) more than they trust them. Police officers are generally fine with tourists, though, and they're good for filing insurance forms if you get robbed — especially in Rio, a city economically tied to its tourism trade.

Here's what you can tell the **polícia** if you want to report a robbery:

- ✔ **Fui roubado/a.** (*fwee* hoh-*bah*-doh/dah; I've been robbed.)

- ✔ **Eu preciso fazer um boletim de ocorrência.** (*eh*-ooh pdeh-*see*-zoo fah-*zeh* oong boh-leh-*ching* jee oh-koh-*hen*-see-ah; I need to report a robbery.)

> ✔ **É para a minha companhia de seguros.** (*eh pah*-dah ah *ming*-yah kom-pahn-*yee*-ah jee seh-*goo*-dohz; It's for my insurance company.)

The **polícia** may ask you some of the following questions:

> ✔ **Quando aconteceu?** (*kwahn*-doh ah-kohn-teh-*seh*-ooh; When did it happen?)
>
> ✔ **Onde aconteceu?** (ah-*ohn*-jee ah-kohn-teh-*seh*-ooh; Where did it happen?)
>
> ✔ **O que que foi roubado?** (ooh *kee* kee *foh*-ee hoh-*bah*-doh; What was stolen?)
>
> ✔ **Viu o assaltante?** (*vee*-ooh ooh ah-sah-ooh-*tahn*-chee; Did you see the assailant?)
>
> ✔ **Usou uma arma?** (ooh-*zoh* ooh-mah *ah*-mah; Did he use a weapon?)

Of course, the **polícia** will probably ask you the regular questions outlined in earlier chapters, like **Qual é seu nome?** (*kwah*-ooh *eh* seh-ooh *noh*-mee; What's your name?) and **Você é de que país?** (voh-*seh* eh jee *kee* pah-*eez*; What country are you from?). (See Chapter 4.)

Although **Socorro!** (soh-*koh*-hoo) means "Help!" Brazilians don't use the verb **socorrer** much. You can also shout **Ajuda!** if you're in trouble, though **Socorro!** is the classic plea for help.

Handling Health Emergencies

Having to get medical treatment in another country can be scary, and it's never fun. Knowing a few phrases that can help you communicate is bound to calm you down a bit!

Getting sick

Here are some helpful phrases to use, whether you're at the **médico** (*meh*-jee-koo; doctor) or the **farmácia** (fah-*mah*-see-ah; drugstore):

- ✔ **Estou com dor de cabeça.** (eh-*stoh* koh-oong *doh* jee kah-*beh*-sah; I have a headache.)

- ✔ **Estou com muita dor.** (eh-*stoh* koh-oong moh-ee-tah *doh;* I'm in a lot of pain.)

- ✔ **Tenho dores no corpo.** (*tang*-yoh *doh*-deez noh *koh*-poo; I have body aches.)

- ✔ **Tenho tosse.** (*tang*-yoh *toh*-see; I have a cough.)

- ✔ **Sou diabético.** (soh jee-ah-*beh*-chee-koh; I'm diabetic.)

- ✔ **Tenho asma.** (*tang*-yoh *ahz*-mah; I have asthma.)

- ✔ **Tem band-aids?** (*tang* bahn-*day*-ee-jeez; Do you have Band-Aids?)

- ✔ **Tem aspirina?** (*tang* ah-spee-*dee*-nah; Do you have aspirin?)

- ✔ **Tem algo para diarréia?** (*tang* ah-ooh-goh *pah*-dah jee-ah-*hay*-ah; Do you have something for diarrhea?)

Other ailments include

- ✔ **resfriado** (hehs-fdee-*ah*-doo; cold)

- ✔ **dor** (doh; pain)

- ✔ **ressaca** (heh-*sah*-kah; hangover)

- ✔ **a malária** (ah mah-*lah*-dee-ah; malaria)

- ✔ **a dengue** (ah *dehn*-gee; dengue fever)

- ✔ **a gripe** (ah *gdee*-pee; the flu)

Here are some questions the pharmacist or doctor may ask you:

- ✔ **Dói?** (*doh*-ee; Does it hurt?)

- ✔ **Onde dói?** (*ohn*-jee *doh*-ee; Where does it hurt?)

- ✔ **Tem febre?** (*tang feh*-bdee; Do you have a fever?)

✔ **Tem náuseas?** (*tang nah*-ooh-zee-ahz; Are you nauseous?)

✔ **É alérgico?** (eh ah-*leh*-zhee-koh; Are you allergic?)

✔ **Tem alta pressão sanguínea?** (tang *ah*-ooh-tah pdeh-*sah*-ooh sahn-*gee*-neh-ah; Do you have high blood pressure?)

✔ **Já foi operado?** (*zhah foh*-ee oh-peh-*dah*-doh; Have you ever had surgery?)

✔ **Abre a boca, por favor.** (*ah*-bdee ah *boh*-kah, poh fah-*voh*; Open your mouth, please.)

✔ **Tome esses comprimidos.** (*toh*-mee *eh*-seez kohm-pdee-*mee*-dooz; Take these pills.)

Here's an example of a conversation you might have at a pharmacy:

Mauricio: **Por favor, estou com o olho inchado.** (poh fah-*voh*, eh-*stoh* koh-oong ooh *ohl*-yoh een-*shah*-doo; Excuse me, I have a swollen eye.)

Pharmacist: **Sabe por que está inchado?** (*sah*-bee poh *keh* eh-*stah* een-*shah*-doo?; Do you know why it's swollen?)

Mauricio: **Não. Acordei hoje e já estava assim.** (*nah*-ooh. ah-koh-*day oh*-zhee ee *zhah* eh-*stah*-vah ah-*sing*; No. I woke up this morning and it was already like that.)

Pharmacist: **Não parece muito grave.** (*nah*-ooh pah-*deh*-see moh-*ee*-toh *gdah*-vee; It doesn't look very serious.)

Mauricio: **O que recomenda fazer?** (ooh *kee* heh-koh-*men*-dah fah-*zeh?*; What do you recommend I do?)

Pharmacist: **Eu recomendo você colocar um saquinho de gelo em cima.** (*eh*-ooh heh-koh-*mehn*-doo voh-*seh* koh-loh-*kah* oong sah-*king*-yoh jee *zheh*-loh ang *see*-mah; I recommend that you put a little bag of ice on it.)

Mauricio: **Mas é normal o olho inchar, sem fazer nada?** (*mah*-eez *eh* noh-*mah*-ooh ooh *ohl*-yoh een-*shah*, *sang* fah-*zeh* nah-dah?; But is it normal for an eye to swell, without doing anything?)

Pharmacist: **Poderia ser uma picada de inseto.** (poh-deh-*dee*-ah *seh* ooh-mah pee-*kah*-dah jee een-*seh*-toh; It could be an insect bite.)

Words to Know

olho inchado	<u>ohl</u>-yoh een-<u>shah</u>-doo	swollen eye
Sabe . . . ?	<u>sah</u>-bee	Do you know . . . ?
já	zhah	already
assim	ah-<u>sing</u>	like that
grave	<u>gdah</u>-vee	serious
colocar	koh-loh-<u>kah</u>	to put
saquinho	sah-<u>king</u>-yoh	little bag
gelo	<u>zheh</u>-loh	ice
inchar	een-<u>shah</u>	to swell
sem	sang	without
Poderia ser . . .	poh-deh-<u>dee</u>-ah <u>seh</u>. . .	It could be
picada	pee-<u>kah</u>-dah	bite
inseto	een-<u>seh</u>-too	insect

Handling broken bones and other injuries

Whether you have a stomach virus or a broken leg, knowing what certain parts of the body are called in Portuguese is useful so you can more easily communicate with doctors in Brazil. I start with **a cabeça** (ah kah-*beh*-sah; the head) and work my way down **o corpo** (ooh *koh*-poo; the body):

- **olho** (*ohl*-yoh; eye)
- **boca** (*boh*-kah; mouth)
- **língua** (*ling*-gwah; tongue)
- **orelha** (oh-*deh*-ooh-yah; ear)
- **nariz** (nah-*deez;* nose)
- **rosto** (*hoh*-stoo; face)
- **dentes** (*dang*-cheez; teeth)
- **sobrancelhas** (soh-bdan-*sel*-yahz; eyebrows)
- **pescoço** (peh-*skoh*-soo; neck)
- **costas** (*koh*-stahz; back)
- **peito** (*pay*-too; chest)
- **braços** (*bdah*-sooz; arms)
- **dedos** (*deh*-dooz; fingers)
- **bumbum** (boong-*boong;* bottom)
- **barriga** (bah-*hee*-gah; belly)
- **pernas** (*peh*-nahz; legs)
- **joelhos** (zhoh-*el*-yoh; knees)
- **pés** (pez; feet)
- **dedos do pé** (*deh*-dooz doo *peh;* toes)

And here are the names of some internal organs and useful medical terms:

- **coração** (koh-dah-*sah*-ooh; heart)
- **pulmões** (pool-*moh*-eez; lungs)
- **intestinos** (een-tehs-*chee*-nooz; intestines)

✔ **fígado** (*fee*-gah-doo; liver)

✔ **sangue** (*sahn*-gee; blood)

✔ **cirurgia** (see-doo-*zhee*-ah; surgery)

Here's a conversation you might have with a doctor after breaking a leg:

Doctor: **Tem dores na perna?** (tang *doh*-deez nah *peh*-nah?; Your leg hurts?)

João: **Sim, dói muito.** (*sing*, *doh*-ee moh-*ee*-toh; Yes, it hurts a lot.)

Doctor: **Vamos fazer uma radiografia.** (*vah*-mohz fah-*zeh* ooh-mah hah-jee-ooh-gdah-*fee*-ah; We're going to take an X-ray.)

João: **Acha que está quebrado?** (*ah*-shah kee eh-*stah* keh-*bdah*-doo?; Do you think it's broken?)

Doctor: **Não sei ainda.** (*nah*-ooh *say* ah-*een*-dah; I don't know yet.)

João: **Vai ter que dar anestesia?** (*vah*-ee *teh* kee *dah* ah-neh-steh-*zee*-ah?; Are you going to have to give me anesthesia?)

Doctor: **Não, não é preciso.** (*nah*-ooh, *nah*-ooh *eh* pdeh-*see*-zoo; No, that's not necessary.)

Words to Know

sala de emergência	<u>sah</u>-lah jee eh-meh-<u>zhang</u>-see-ah	emergency room
ambulância	ahm-boo-<u>lahn</u>-see-ah	ambulance
hospitais	oh-spee-<u>tah</u>-eez	hospitals
uma radiografia	ooh-mah hah-jee-ooh-gdah-<u>fee</u>-ah	X-ray

quebrada	keh-<u>bdah</u>-dah	broken
ainda	ah-<u>een</u>-dah	yet/still
Vai ter que . . . ?	<u>vah</u>-ee <u>teh</u> kee	Will you have to . . . ?
dar	dah	to give
anestesia	ah-neh-steh-<u>zee</u>-ah	anesthesia

Discussing Legal Problems

Misunderstandings with the police can occur. If the situation is at all **sério** (*seh*-dee-ooh; serious), the first thing to do is contact the nearest consulate for your country. You may also need to contact an **advogado** (*ahj*-voh-*gah*-doo; lawyer). In that case, ask for one who speaks English:

- ✔ **Tem um advogado que fala inglês?** (*tang* oong ahj-voh-*gah*-doh kee *fah*-lah een-*glehz;* Is there a lawyer who speaks English?)

- ✔ **Tem um consulado americano aqui?** (*tang* oong kohn-soo-*lah*-doh ah-meh-dee-*kah*-noh ah-*kee*; Is there an American consulate here?)

With any luck, you won't ever have to say or hear these phrases:

- ✔ **Quero fazer uma queixa.** (*keh*-doo fah-*zeh* ooh-mah *kay*-shah; I want to register a complaint.)

- ✔ **Vamos ter que dar uma multa.** (*vah*-mohz *teh* kee *dah* ooh-mah *mool*-tah; We're going to have to give you a ticket.)

✔ **Vamos te levar para a delegacia de polícia.**
(*vah*-mohz chee leh-*vah pah*-dah ah deh-leh-gah-*see*-ah jee poh-*lee*-see-ah; We're going to take you to the police station.)

You want to **evitar** (eh-vee-*tah;* avoid) a visit to **a cadeia** (ah kah-*day*-ah; jail) at all costs — jails in Brazil are notoriously overcrowded, scary places.

Chapter 12

Ten Favorite Brazilian Portuguese Expressions

• •

*B*razilian Portuguese is a fun language. It's humorous and full of spice and emotion. Think of these phrases as clues to Brazilian culture. They start to paint a picture of a nation full of lively, friendly, and laid-back people.

Que saudade!

The word **saudade** (sah-ooh-*dah*-jee) has no direct translation in English, and it's a major source of linguistic pride for Brazilians. Use **Que saudade!** (kee sah-ooh-*dah*-jee) when you miss something so desperately, you have a heartache over it. People say **Que saudade!** when they remember their best friend who's now living far away, or their childhood beach.

Fala sério!

Say **Fala sério** (*fah*-lah *seh*-dee-oh) to mean "You're kidding!" or "You're joking!" or "No way!" Brazilians also say **Não acredito!** (*nah*-ooh ah-kdeh-*jee*-toh; I can't believe it!) in the same situations. But **Fala sério** has a funnier tone to it. It literally means, "Talk seriously."

. . . pra caramba!

Here's a great way to emphasize how off-the-charts something is. **Pra caramba** (pdah kah-*dahm*-bah) is most often used at the end of a sentence to exaggerate something. Use this phrase instead of putting **muito** (moh-*ee*-toh; very) or **bem** (bang; very) in front of these same words.

Take the classic phrase **É boa pra caramba** (eh *boh*-ah pdah kah-*dahm*-bah). **Boa** by itself means "good." When **pra caramba** comes after *good,* it transforms *It's good* to *It's amazing.*

Engraçado means "funny." **Engraçado pra caramba** (ang-gdah-*sah*-doo pdah kah-*dahm*-bah) means "hilarious." **Muito frio** means "very cold." So how cold was it? **Frio pra caramba!** (*fdee*-oh pdah kah-*dahm*-bah; Really, really cold!).

Lindo maravilhoso!

Lindo maravilhoso! (*leen*-doh mah-dah-veel-*yoh*-zoo) is a very Brazilian saying that literally translates to "Beautiful, marvelous!" Brazilians like to gush about beauty and how amazing things are.

The weather can be **lindo maravilhoso! — Hoje estava um dia lindo maravilhoso!** (*oh*-zhee eh-*stah*-vah oong *jee*-ah *leen*-doh mah-dah-veel-*yoh*-zoo; Today the weather was fantastic!). A place can be **lindo maravilhoso! — O local é lindo maravilhoso!** (ooh loh-*kah*-ooh eh *leen*-doh mah-dah-veel-*yoh*-zoo; The place is amazing!). If you admire someone's work, that can be **lindo maravilhoso!,** too.

And try to remember to use an *a* at the end of each word instead of the *o* if the word you're talking about is feminine. A gorgeous woman is **linda maravilhosa!** And a handsome man is **lindo maravilhoso!**

É mesmo?

É mesmo? (eh *mehz*-moh) means "Really?" It's usually used to react to some interesting new fact.

You tell someone: Did you know that Portuguese is the fifth most-spoken language in the world? She answers back: **É mesmo?**

You tell someone that you're learning Portuguese. What does she answer back? Sometimes it's an enthusiastic **É mesmo!** (Really!).

Um beijo! or Um abraço!

Brazilians are very affectionate people. They often end a conversation with a friend or acquaintance they feel friendly toward by saying **Um beijo!** (oong *bay*-zhoh; a kiss) or **Um abraço!** (oong ah-*bdah*-soh; a hug). In general, women use **Um beijo!** to male and female friends, and men use **Um beijo!** to women and **Um abraço!** to male friends. These expressions are also common ways to end e-mails.

Imagina!

Brazilians are also very hospitable. After telling you "thank you" — **obrigado** (oh-bdee-*gah*-doh) if you're male and **obrigada** (oh-bdee-*gah*-dah) if you're female — a Brazilian often says **Imagina!** (mah-*zhee*-nah; *Literally:* Imagine!) to mean "It's no trouble at all!" The initial *i* is chopped off in spoken language. It sounds like **Magina!**

Pois não?

Here's a common phrase you may hear when you enter a shop or call a service-oriented company over the phone, like a restaurant. **Pois não?** (*poh*-eez *nah*-ooh) means "Can I help you?" It's a funny phrase, because it literally means "Because no?" It's pretty nonsensical, and Brazilians have a hard time saying where the phrase originated.

Com certeza!

This is another fun, common phrase. **Com certeza!** (koh-oong seh-*teh*-zah; *Literally:* With certainty!) translates to "Of course!" or "Definitely!"

If someone asks you **Vai para a festa?** (*vah*-ee pah-dah ah *fehs*-tah; Are you going to the party?), you can answer **Com certeza!**

Fique tranqüilo

If Brazilians value any single trait, it's optimism, being able to solve problems. And if the problem can't be fixed, just relax and forget about it. At the first signs of someone's stress, a Brazilian often says **Fique tranqüilo** (*fee*-kee kdang-*kwee*-loh; Don't worry). It has a very calming effect.

If the bus takes off just as you arrive at the bus stop, **fique tranqüilo**: There'll be another one in ten minutes. And you can make friends while you wait.

Chapter 13

Ten Phrases That Make You Sound Like a Local

. . . .

*P*eople often say that Brazilian Portuguese is lyrical. Following are some of the nuts and bolts of the language that help to give it its sound. Using these little words can make you sound really fluent in Portuguese!

Né?

Brazilians probably say **né** (neh) more often than any other word or term. It means "Right?" They stick it at the end of sentences all the time: **Você vai para o aeroporto amanhã, né?** (voh-*seh vah*-ee pah-dah ooh ah-eh-doh-*poh*-too ah-mahn-*yah, neh;* You're going to the airport tomorrow, right?)

And you may also hear **né** in the middle of sentences, where it doesn't really have any use or meaning: **Eu vi o meu amigo, né, e depois não lembro de mais nada** (*eh*-ooh *vee* ooh *meh*-ooh ah-*mee*-goh neh ee deh-*poh*-eez *nah*-ooh *lehm*-bdoh jee mah-eez *nah*-dah; I saw my friend, right, and then I don't remember anything else).

Né is the short way of saying **não é?** (*nah*-ooh *eh;* Literally: is it not?).

Tá

You know when you're listening to someone talking on the phone, and you hear them say, "Oh . . . Yeah . . . Right . . . Uh-huh . . ."? **Tá** (tah) is the Brazilian equivalent of these words. If someone's giving you directions on how to get somewhere, for example, you can repeat **Tá . . . Tá . . . Tá . . .** and it'll sound like you're understanding and recording into memory everything he's saying.

Tá is the short way of saying **Está** (eh-*stah*).

Ah é?

Ah é (ah *eh*) is one of a few ways to say "Really?" It's also another of those phone conversation fillers. You can use it either to say "Really?" with real interest in what the person's saying or as a way to show the speaker you haven't fallen asleep.

Então

Então (eh-*tah*-ooh; so/then) is a major conversation filler in Brazil. People often say **então** to change the subject to something more interesting when there's a lull in a conversation. It also can be used to simply say "so" or "then."

Sabe?

Here's a case where the translation and use of the word is exactly the same as in English. A Brazilian's saying **Sabe?** (*sah*-bee) is the equivalent of an American speaker's weaving the phrase *You know?* constantly throughout.

Imagine two people talking on the phone. Person A is telling a story to Person B. Person A says **Sabe?** about every 20 seconds as he talks. What does Person B say? (See previous entries for clues): **Tá . . . Ah é? . . . Tá. . . .**

Meio

Meio (*may*-o; sort of) is an easy term for you to practice and wow native speakers with. Just remember — the pronunciation sounds like *mayo* in English (yes, the short way of saying *mayonnaise*).

Use **meio** when you'd say "sort of":

> ✔ **Ele é meio alto.** (*eh*-lee *eh may*-oh *ah*-ooh-*toh*-ooh; He's sort of tall.)

> ✔ **O vestido parece meio asiático.** (ooh vehs-*chee*-doo pah-*deh*-see *may*-oh ah-zee-*ah*-chee-koh; The dress looks sort of Asian.)

Ou seja/E tal

These two phrases are pure fillers. **Ou seja** (ooh *seh*-zhah) means "in other words" but is often used by speakers just to gather their thoughts for a few seconds. And **e tal** (ee *tah*-ooh) means "et cetera" or "and stuff like that" or "and everything."

Here is a real example of **e tal** I found on Google in Brazilian Portuguese (www.google.com.br): **O livro é sobre dragões e tal** (ooh *leev*-doh eh *sob*-dee drah-*goh*-eez ee *tah*-ooh; The book is about dragons and stuff like that).

Cê Instead of Você

Here's an important one. People very often shorten **você** (voh-*seh;* you) to **cê** when they speak. Instead of **Você entendeu?, Você vai agora?,** or **Você é de onde?** they say

✔ **Cê entendeu?** (seh en-ten-*deh*-ooh; Did you understand?)

✔ **Cê vai agora?** (seh *vah*-ee ah-*goh*-dah; Are you leaving now?)

✔ **Cê é de onde?** (seh *eh* jee *ohn*-jee; Where are you from?)

Pra Instead of Para a

Para (*pah*-dah) means "for" or "in order to." Sometimes Brazilians pronounce **para** as **pra** (pdah).

✔ **Vai pra praia?** (*vah*-ee *pdah pdah*-eeh-ah; Are you going to the beach?)

✔ **Pra fazer o quê?** (*pdah fah-zeh ooh keh;* To do what?)

Tô instead of Estou

Estou (eh-*stoh*; I am) is often shortened to **tô,** both in spoken speech and in e-mails.

✔ **Tô com fome.** (*toh* koh-oong *foh*-mee; I'm hungry.)

✔ **Hoje tô feliz.** (*oh*-zhee toh feh-*leez;* Today I'm happy.)

Index